fractured land

fractured land

THE PRICE OF INHERITING OIL

LISA WESTBERG PETERS

MINNESOTA
HISTORICAL
SOCIETY PRESS

www.mnhspress.org
The Minnesota Historical Society Press is a member of the Association of American University Presses.

Manufactured in the United States of America

10 9 8 7 6 5 4 3 2 1

∞ The paper used in this publication meets the minimum requirements of the American National Standard for Information Sciences—Permanence for Printed Library Materials, ANSI Z39.48–1984.

International Standard Book Number
ISBN: 978-0-87351-952-6 (paper)
ISBN: 978-0-87351-953-3 (e-book)

Library of Congress Cataloging-in-Publication Data
Peters, Lisa Westberg.
    Fractured land : the price of inheriting oil / Lisa Westberg Peters.
      pages cm
    Summary: "An avowed environmentalist discovers she will inherit mineral rights and oil royalties from land once owned by her grandfather. In exploring her family's history and the mining industry in North Dakota, she comes to see shades of gray in issues of conservation and development that once seemed black and white"— Provided by publisher.
    Includes bibliographical references.
    ISBN 978-0-87351-952-6 (paperback) — ISBN 978-0-87351-953-3 (ebook)
    1. Oil fields—North Dakota—Williston Region. 2. Petroleum engineering—Environmental aspects—North Dakota—Williston Region.
    3. Land tenure—North Dakota—Williston Region. 4. Peters, Lisa Westberg—Homes and haunts. 5. Williston (N.D.)—History. I. Title.
    TN872.N9P48 2014
    333.8'23150978473—dc23
                                                                            2014024057

This and other Minnesota Historical Society Press books are available from popular e-book vendors.

For my father, my uncle Rich, and Dave

fractured land

fractured land

CONTRACT

An agreement between two or more parties creating obligations that are enforceable or otherwise recognizable at law.
BLACK'S LAW DICTIONARY, TENTH EDITION

A contract involves an exchange of promises and benefits. Oil and gas leases are considered legal contracts.

MINNEAPOLIS

It's the middle of the night. I press the power button on my computer. I'm looking for something, anything, to divert my thoughts from the fact that my father is dying.

When my home page finally fills my screen and the whirly rainbow stops whirling, I go to a dignified website that might put amateur insomniacs back to sleep. Not me. The State Historical Society of North Dakota site has scads of old photos. I love old photos. More importantly, my father, a native North Dakotan, also loves them.

I click through until a search window pops up. Now what? I don't even know exactly what I'm searching for. It's 2 AM and complex thought usually requires coffee, so I type in just one word: Westberg. It was my grandfather's last name, my father's last name. In response to the prompt, several photos pop up. Now I'm awake.

Two of the photos are of my long-dead grandfather, Oscar Westberg, and several other middle-aged Williston, North Dakota, community leaders gathered around tables. Another is of the Williston Junior Municipal Band with my dad on clarinet and his brother on tuba. A few other photos seem irrelevant.

But two photos show a sleek, post–World War II sedan next to a makeshift oil-drilling rig, a structure that Don Quixote could have beaten in a jousting match had he wandered

1

across time and space to the twentieth century and the American plains. There are a few pickup trucks, which probably belonged to the drill crew, and the horizon is flat.

Not only does Dad love old photos, he loves North Dakota oil. From my grandfather, he inherited farmland and mineral rights, a potential cash cow that for decades was more like a cash gopher. Dad's home state used to be known for durum wheat and silence; today it's known for truck traffic, mile-long oil trains, and booming production of petroleum crude.

I'm awake, but I still don't know what to make of the caption: *Westberg oil well somewhere in North Dakota, 1954.* Were the photos taken on my grandfather's wheat farm? Do oil com-

panies name oil wells after the landowner? And who's William Shemorry, the guy who took the photo?

I print out the photos because Dad will adore them, and I plan to fly to Florida to see him next week, on Tuesday, the same day as my sister.

Swimming comes easily enough for me that I can obsess about all kinds of things without ever worrying about drowning. And they say it's the best overall exercise. But that's only if your dad isn't dying and you're not spiraling yourself into the ground with stress.

This time, swimming turns out to be the best overall way to achieve muscle cramps. My right foot cramps up, then the left foot, then my right calf, which has never happened before. Maybe stress is having a direct effect on my muscles. Why wouldn't it? Or maybe swimming is bad for you and the studies proving this fact haven't been published yet.

I've taken a few meditation classes at Zen centers, but the moment I remember to pay attention to my breathing always comes as a complete surprise. *Oh! I should just pay attention to my breathing, and that will trick my muscles into relaxing!*

This is not the way the Zen Buddhists would put it. They might say something like, *Just be still and know.* Today those words don't work for me.

THIRTY-FIVE THOUSAND FEET OVER THE MIDWEST
How are you supposed to behave while flying across the country to watch your father die? I think I'm acting like a normal person, but I feel like a stretched-out sock with rocks rolling

Mid-1950s oil-drilling derrick and gas flare on my grandfather's farm near Tioga, North Dakota. William Shemorry/State Historical Society of North Dakota

around inside. If my face were showing this tumult, the flight attendants would be leaning across my seatmate and asking me probing questions.

When my sister and I heard this morning—three days before our scheduled flight—that Dad had stopped eating and drinking, we both caught the next flights out, she from Denver, I from Minneapolis. Both of us were scheduled to arrive in Gainesville, Florida, around midnight. My two brothers were also hastily making their own arrangements to arrive soon after that. My father's only surviving brother, Richard, who hates to fly, was booking a flight from Pennsylvania to Florida.

It's after 5 PM. I choose a socially acceptable way to behave: I order a glass of red wine. If it had been any PM, I probably would have opted for a glass of red wine. I don't flinch at the price, whatever it is.

I pour some of the wine into a plastic cup and take a sip. My father has long talked about his lingering connections to the harsh landscape of his childhood, the land he left behind decades ago. After his father died, Dad was named executor of his father's estate, but he never wanted the worries of farming. What's the price of wheat this year? How much damage did the hail do?

And then there was the oil. He was always telling us how hard it was to find—many drilling efforts came up empty—and expensive to pursue because the oil formations were so damn deep. Oil prices needed to be high enough to justify drilling costs, and even then, drillers might not find oil.

But that whole hard-to-find thing? It's all so 1990s. Today, drillers are able to aim straight down for two miles until they reach the layers of shale containing the oil, and then they turn their drills sideways and drill for another two miles through the heart of those layers.

Drillers then inject water, sand, and chemicals into the well at high pressure to fracture the dense, or tight, rock, forming escape routes for the oil and gas. This wickedly effective combination of horizontal drilling and hydraulic fracturing—fracking—might allow my father to finally hit it big, or at least hit it.

In recent years, he could barely contain his excitement. His letters were filled with exclamation points. *Hoo boy! Here's hoping!*

My dad has always been in charge of keeping track of the confusing business of North Dakota oil. My siblings and I never paid much attention. There was precious little to pay attention to. And none of us understands the *lingua franca* of the industry: oil leases, the complex legal agreements between the people who own the minerals and the companies that want to extract them. Mom was always within earshot of Dad's frequent conversations with his brother Rich, but North Dakota oil was definitely Dad's thing.

Oil wasn't my dad's only obsession. A son of the treeless plains, he also came to love trees. He never got misty-eyed about their pretty leaves. Instead he had an engineer's admiration for the way their roots could help solve a problem he had: an unstable riverbank. When we were kids, we helped him plant hundreds of pines near our A-frame cabin overlooking the St. Croix River in western Wisconsin.

I gulp down the last of the airplane-grade wine and write an airplane-grade haiku for my dad:

pine seedlings anchor
the sandy soil of a bluff—
soft spring rains soak in

GAINESVILLE, FLORIDA
I enter the front door of the hospice.

There are three things I want to do while I'm here, and these things decrease exponentially in importance with their position on the list:

1. I want to touch my dad, his arm, his forehead. If he isn't

conscious any longer, maybe he'll feel the warmth and pressure of my hand.

2. I want to tell him I love him. Of course.

3. I want to show him those damn oil well photos. They're tucked into my backpack.

When I think how much he loved in his later years to toddle out to the mailbox to see if there was an oil royalty check—even a tiny one, and they were always tiny—I feel as though I packed well for this trip: two oil well photos with the word "Westberg" in the captions and a few changes of clothes.

I've never entered a hospice before. Silk flower arrangements. Mauves, blues, greens in the furniture and on the walls. Kind of quiet, actually very quiet, but not creepy. There's art in the hallway, some of it created by local people. Maybe their loved ones died here? Ahead, there's a nurses' station at the intersection of two hallways.

Walter Westberg? I ask.

The nurses smile and point the way.

My pace drops off a cliff as I realize his room is not that far away. In fact, it's only a few feet away. On the right. And the door is open. My mother will be here, too.

My back prickles with the professionally casual gaze of the nurses behind me. I walk in.

My nose registers no offending odors. It's like entering a hospital room. But nobody scurries in with IVs and thermometers and meds. Nobody scurries out with samples of bodily fluids. Nobody scurries for any reason.

At my father's bedside, with her knitting on her lap, is my mother. She smiles, and I breathe out. Didn't realize I'd been holding my breath. One huge source of my mother's anxiety—uncertainty—is gone. Dad's here. We all know he's dying, and it won't be long.

He lies on a hospital-style bed. He's been more and more

frail in recent years, but now he's very thin, and his forearms are dark with hemorrhages. *He insisted on taking an aspirin a day!* Mom says with the exasperated voice that comes from years of living with someone. It's not that I had doubted Dad was dying; I didn't. But knowing and seeing are two different things.

I touch his arm. It's warm. It's still my father.

Dad, I say.

He opens his eyes, and as much as this is possible when you're only a day and a half away from death, his whole face smiles.

I love you, Dad, I say. My voice is strong, and I smile, too, marveling at my previously undemonstrated capacity for turning off the tears when it's clear that tears are counterproductive.

With an urgency that must come from lying on your deathbed, Dad tells me he loves me, too. His voice is barely there, but neither of us bothers with apologies, conditions, or yeah-buts. We love each other. Period.

My sister has followed me into the room and greets him in precisely the same way. I pull my mom aside.

Has he said anything since you got here? I ask.

She has to think. *Not much,* she says. *But he knows he's dying.*

How could you tell . . . if he didn't say much? I ask.

He did this. She does a thumbs-down.

Uncle Rich calls, says he missed his flight and has booked another one. After my brothers arrive, all six of us—my parents and the four of us kids—occupy the same room, a rare occurrence. As we hold Dad's hand, stroke his arm and his forehead, we gradually downshift from the rhythm of cross-country travel to the rhythm of Dad's labored but steady breathing.

Remember his instructions for starting up the pump at the cabin?

The ancient pump was pieced together from scrounged parts, and Dad's instructions were twenty steps long. Step four was something like, "You've just begun." Good God. Dad never, ever bought new when there was a chance he could fix old. It was a North Dakota Great Depression thing. He knew it; we all knew it.

Remember how we used to brag about his cold weather mask?

At 3M, Dad's employer in St. Paul for thirty years, scientists were required to devote fifteen percent of their time to tinkering with their own ideas. Sanctioned tinkering! It was an inventor's paradise. Somehow—I don't know how—Dad's tinkering resulted in a new and improved bra cup made of a special nonwoven fabric. I don't like to think of the water cooler conversations that resulted in this new product, which he and a colleague patented in 1962.

Five years later, he and a co-inventor received one of 3M's first patents for a disposable face mask made of nonwoven fabric; further tinkering by many staff scientists resulted in an explosion of nonwoven products. My mother wore Dad's cold weather mask when she was stripping the paint off old dressers and tables. I might have worn one as part of a Halloween costume.

Rain. He loved rain!

My father hated drought, but it was more than that. He hated when it hadn't rained for just a few days. In his letters, celebration of rain or despair over the lack of it often came in the first paragraph: *I'm happy to report that our drowth is over. We've had inches of rain, nearly up to normal for July. The fires in central Florida are almost gone or under control. What a relief.*

Fear and loathing of dry weather. That was a North Dakota Dust Bowl thing. Even the word "drowth" felt like a Great Plains thing.

And of course the oil. He loved the oil.

He especially loved the idea that his godforsaken home state of North Dakota might someday come through for him. He had a cocktail napkin that said:

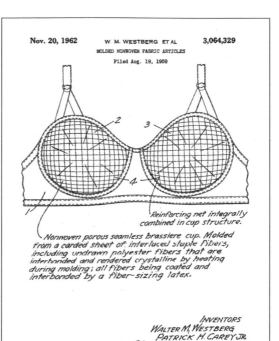

Nov. 20, 1962   W. M. WESTBERG ET AL   3,064,329

MOLDED NONWOVEN FABRIC ARTICLES

Filed Aug. 19, 1959

Reinforcing net integrally combined in cup structure.

Nonwoven porous seamless brassiere cup. Molded from a carded sheet of interlaced staple fibers, including undrawn polyester fibers that are interbonded and rendered crystalline by heating during molding; all fibers being coated and interbonded by a fiber-sizing latex.

INVENTORS
WALTER M. WESTBERG
PATRICK H. CAREY JR.
BY
Carpenter, Abbott, Coulter & Kinney
ATTORNEYS

My father was awarded his first patent in 1962 and spent his career as an inventor for 3M. U.S. Patent Office illustration

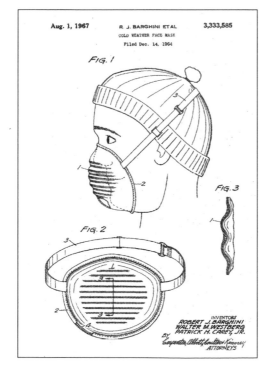

Aug. 1, 1967   R. J. BARGHINI ET AL   3,333,585

COLD WEATHER FACE MASK

Filed Dec. 14, 1964

FIG. 1

FIG. 3

FIG. 2

INVENTORS
ROBERT J. BARGHINI
WALTER M. WESTBERG
PATRICK H. CAREY, JR.
BY
Carpenter, Abbott, Coulter & Kinney
ATTORNEYS

One of 3M's first disposable face masks made of nonwoven fabric, my father, co-inventor, 1967. U.S. Patent Office illustration

SECRET TO SUCCESS
Rise Early
Work Late
Strike Oil!

The successful combination of horizontal drilling and hydraulic fracturing had jump-started the weekly phone conversations with Uncle Rich, also a mineral rights owner who profited when a well started producing.

Did you get your check for the new well on section so-and-so? They say the Bakken is going to produce for years and years. Wouldn't Dad be pleased with the way things are going now?

Memories of my father float around the room like pillow feathers, and with each heavy breath, Dad keeps them aloft and alive.

I open my backpack.

Dad, look.

Can he hear me? Are his hearing aids in? How can I feel so confused when the situation here is so simple?

I sit at his bedside and hold up one of the photos I found on the historical society's website, the sepia-toned photo of the oil-drilling derrick from about sixty years ago. It's just a crappy printout on a plain sheet of paper produced at two in the morning on a cheap inkjet printer. I hold it a few feet from his face at eye level.

My dad may be dying, but at the sight of this iconic symbol of oil, his eyes widen and his eyebrows shoot skyward. His toothy smile broadens into wide-open pleasure. It doesn't matter whose oil well this is.

When he smiles, all I feel is contentment.

This is no time for me to bring up my discomfort with the fracking-induced oil boom. I'm happy for my father and his growing oil checks, but I consider myself an environmentalist.

My environmental consciousness began in that unconscious blur of childhood. When you're a kid and you hear a whippoorwill whippoorwilling every single night somewhere in the woods, at first it's just a curiosity, and then it becomes part of your day. With time, your sense of what a day ought to include turns into conscious affection for those crazy whippoorwills, and that affection fosters a desire to protect the places where whippoorwills hang out.

By the time I entered college, Americans were demanding legislation to clean up our air and water and I was watching and listening. Later I studied geology, and my reading took a tilt toward Stephen Jay Gould. He showed me in essay after essay the intimate connection between the history of life and the history of the earth; it wasn't much of a leap to realize that the future of life—our future—depends on the well-being of the earth's atmosphere and oceans.

When my daughters were growing up, my environmentalism popped out in annoying ways: *No, hon, I'm not going to drive you to school. There's a bus! You can take the bus.*

But that label "environmentalist," it's as imprecise as the term "vegetarian," which embraces everybody from butter haters to fish lovers. If environmentalists range from bomb throwing to armchair, I fall into the latter category: I turn off lights when I leave a room, buy fuel-efficient cars, and recycle everything my city wants me to recycle, but I tend to leave my love of clean air and clean water behind whenever I pack for a trip. Off I go in fossil-fueled cars and planes with my growing collection of electronic devices.

When my father dies, my mother will inherit his mineral rights. Eventually my siblings and I will inherit hers. At that point, I will benefit from drilling techniques that require millions of gallons of water, dozens of chemicals, some of them unknown even to regulators, and the safe disposal of toxic wastes.

It would make quite a headline:

Environmentalist Rakes in ND Oil Profits

And so I sit on an uncomfortable fence. On one side is a sea of oil that fouls beaches and birds and contributes to climate mayhem. On the other side is a sea of oil—my family's oil!— that provides jobs for thousands of people, financial breathing room for my parents, and wealth for the long-suffering state of North Dakota.

Nope. You can see, I'm sure, how a hospice room is not exactly the place for that kind of discussion.

My dad sees this picture of an old North Dakota oil well— or it's going to be an oil well as soon as they hit pay dirt—and does a thumbs-up.

BONUS

> The Mineral Owner, in consideration of TEN OR MORE DOLLARS cash in hand, leases exclusively to the Mineral Developer the property described below for the purposes of exploring for, drilling for, and producing oil and/or gas.
>
> *In North Dakota, an oil company (the mineral developer) typically offers a person with mineral rights (the mineral owner) a cash incentive to do business with it. It's a way of saying, "Take a chance on us." The size of the bonus helps the mineral owner decide whether to sign a lease or which company to sign with. The full bonus is rarely specified in the contract.*

GAINESVILLE, FLORIDA

My father died a few days ago, it's almost Christmas, and I'm in the middle of a state known for alligators and concealed weapons. No evergreens dusted with snow, no children sledding, no slushy freeways clogged with pissed-off shoppers hoping to get to the mall before it closes.

Uncle Rich has returned to Pennsylvania. One brother has already gone back to the Twin Cities. My sister and my other brother stand in the parking lot outside my parents'—now just my mother's—apartment. They seem reluctant and, at the same time, itchy to leave. They have planes to catch, but we all stand around, staring at each other. I'm the logical one to stay with Mom because I work as a writing tutor at a state university and the university is on semester break. I don't have to be back at work till mid-January.

It's logical, but do I also have to be chief grief counselor? I don't think I can do that yet. I'm still feeling numb about everything, my confusion about how to talk to a parent with a terminal illness and my whole family's shaky navigation through unfamiliar territory.

Right now, I would much rather curl up and hide, sort through my father's death and the past several months all by myself. But I can't leave Mom alone for Christmas, not after her mate of sixty-two years has just died, not when she can barely walk because her knees are shot, not when she sometimes forgets to turn off the stove, and not when she must be frightened of being truly alone for the first time.

Do unto others. It's just about the only religion I have.

My siblings and I finally exchange quick hugs, a few words, and that's it. They're gone.

My mother may be alone for the first time, but she grew up on those vast windy plains, too. She lost her parents when she was a teenager and for years lived with a guy who had lost many of the warm and fuzzy spousal skills he might have had as a younger man.

My mother doesn't need a babysitter.

So, for the next several days, our routines run on parallel tracks. She gets up early and makes her own breakfast: cold cereal with blueberries and cheap Eight O'Clock coffee. I get up later and make my own breakfast: oatmeal with blueberries and Starbucks.

During the day, Mom knits, does some serious egret-watching on her back porch, and goes through the blizzard of death-related paperwork. I disappear into my father's study to purge his files of useless documents—five-year-old Medicare brochures, ten-year-old insurance promotions—and replace his filing system with something that might make sense to my mother who can knit circles around anyone but has possibly never filed a document in a file drawer.

No grief counseling occurs, but toward evening, our paths cross on the porch.

Tell me what you and Dad did in your courting days, I say. *Music,* she says. *We went to hear great music.*

She talks about the concerts they attended in Minneapolis, remembers the names of the symphonies, the soloists, the concert halls. Their love of music outlived almost everything else—Dad's hearing, her knees, raucous evenings around the card table with friends. When the public radio station in Gainesville dropped its classical music programming, my outraged parents charged into the nearest Radio Shack and bought an HD radio receiver to pull in classical music stations from faraway places.

Dad's office is pretty basic: a filing cabinet, an old computer, a printer, and a desk. I don't expect surprises, but that's what I find.

Lying in the back of one of his desk drawers is something I don't recognize. It's an album—just three inches by five inches—that holds about a hundred old film negatives in transparent folders. Until now, I would have said with some confidence that I had seen all of my dad's photos.

Dad was a serious amateur photographer for most of his life, and he passed along his love of black and white photography to me. I have early memories of going into his darkroom to watch him dodge and burn and mask, all before Photoshop computerized those processes.

In careful printing—a sure indication that Dad wrote these words when he was young and still cared about his handwriting—are short descriptions of the black-and-white negatives. I pick one at random. It's labeled "OBERLIN VICTORY—Walt in room." I recognize a young version of my dad, but I almost can't look. It's a goddamn beefcake photo.

My dad must have set up a tripod and taken a photo of himself sitting on a bed, his back resting against the wall (is that the light of a porthole shining on him, is he on a ship?) and

Dad relaxes aboard the Oberlin Victory, *a Merchant Marine ship,
in 1947. Walter Westberg*

his knees up. He's gazing dreamily at the camera with a Mona
Lisa smile on his face. And here's where it starts to get squeamish for a daughter. He's just plain naked except for boxers,
and those appear to be a Hawaiian print, or at the very least,
a splashy print. OK, it's a North Dakota boy beefcake photo.

I don't know exactly when he took it, but he appears to be
in his twenties, a virile young man and, daughterly squeamish-
ness aside, handsome.

In another shot, five young men are sitting in the bleachers
of a grandstand. On the far left is my uncle Rich, about to put
a cigarette in his mouth. One guy gazes through binoculars.
The middle guy stares at a race sheet, cigarette hanging from
his mouth. He wears flashy sunglasses, oversized with a bold
white bar—ramrod straight—across the top and equally bold
white temples. He has slicked-back hair, is clearly someone
with a sense of style. But his socks! They're white, sagging

a bit, and exposed because his foot is propped against the bleacher back in front of him.

Behind them is a grandstand populated by a smattering of horse-racing fans. The men's fedoras and a woman's straw hat give them away as World War II–era racing fans. Nobody is looking at the camera, all of them intent on the race.

And sprinkled throughout this little album are 1940s-style selfies, young men in silly poses and silly clothes, young men at the top of their game, training for military service or just back from serving.

My dad took these photos, but I never knew that man. He must have been full of beans and a little reckless if you judge him by his company (to wit, the guy in the crazy sunglasses). The man I knew had a sense of humor, but reckless? And I never knew him as a portrait photographer. He claimed he wasn't interested in people as subjects. He often aimed his large-format cameras at industrial shapes, textures, and lines—the geometry of pipes and culverts and weathered siding.

But this is a portrait, and I love it.

Uncle Rich, far left, and hometown friends from Williston at a post–World War II Regina, Saskatchewan, horse race. Walter Westberg

I open the lower file drawer and I stop. Oil files. A lot of them. I can tell at a glance that they contain information about the family oil wells in North Dakota, but Dad hadn't organized the files alphabetically by well name. Instead he organized them by location: section 5, section 31.

I pull one out and can't make much sense out of what I'm reading. This is a world I do not know. At all. I would need a lot more than the couple weeks I plan to be in Florida to grasp what I'm seeing.

I plug a brand-new flash drive into his computer. Dad entered the computer age already an old geezer, and he navigated it with rules made slippery by senility, and of course there was the inevitable disconnect between a mind shaped by slide rules and minds shaped by silicon and circuit boards.

But he did all right. He had posted tiny sticky notes everywhere, on the computer monitor, the desk, and the processor. Each pastel-colored square was filled with his chicken scratchings, reminders of what to do, where to turn for help, maybe even what to buy at the grocery store. The whole thing was his private world. He never let Mom touch his computer. He was more generous with his kids, but it wasn't worth the aggravation. He hovered like an old mother hen.

I click through the labyrinthine pathways to his documents, and when I find his list of files, my index finger stops clicking. My dad had seventy-three documents containing stories and articles, some of which he'd successfully published in the local newspaper. I had expected to see those. But each file begins with the same word: my name.

lisa 44
lisa 114
lisa 1153
lisa121
Lisa116

Dad had never said anything to me about his file-naming system. He had always loved to hear about my writing and had always asked me how things were going, but establishing a Lisa-based naming system? Sometimes he capitalized my name, sometimes he didn't. Sometimes he included a space between the name and the number, sometimes not. I wince because my own system of naming files is riddled with such inconsistencies.

I tell myself he was just exhibiting ordinary parental love, but this champion of all oxymorons hits me hard today.

———————————

I have no idea how to pick up cremated remains. It's not that I can't find the funeral home. I'm getting good at finding my way around Gainesville. Even though the University of Florida is here, it feels like a small town.

The traffic is terrible here! my mother says.

Ha! I scoff. *You haven't driven in Minneapolis lately. You should drive 35W at rush hour. And don't forget the potholes. You guys don't have potholes.*

She gratefully concedes this point.

I will be able to find my way to the funeral home. But what happens then? What if I can't make it through the door? In lieu of answers, I make a list. Lists calm me.

—Post office to mail Grandpa memorabilia to the six grandkids

—Grocery store for more blueberries

—Thrift store to drop off Dad's clothes

—Liquor store for a bottle of wine

—Funeral home for ashes

It seems smart to put the funeral home at the end of the list.

An hour and a half of driving around and I'm almost finished. I pull into the parking lot of the liquor store.

The owners have apparently spent nothing on the kinds of things—paint, carpeting, and bright lights—that might make their store more pleasant to enter. Mom recommended this place. She and my dad, seasoned tightwads, were loyal customers because they claimed it was the cheapest liquor store in town. Cheap trumps pleasant any day.

I should be searching the aisles for the wine section, but instead I'm wandering around, barely noticing anything. I call my husband, Dave. My only intent is to say hello even though it's the middle of the workday in Minnesota. Saying hello, that's code for aimless chatter, right? You say a lot more than hello—like, *How's your day?* or *What are we eating for dinner?*—but this time I don't get past hello. I get as far as silence, which contrasts sharply with the scratchy cell phone signal. Radio waves beam from Florida to a satellite and back down to Minnesota.

Are you OK? Dave asks from St. Paul.

I want to tell him I'm a block away from the funeral home. Those words don't come out. And it's weird, but I start to think about all the other customers who have probably cried in this store. Come on. Sometimes people go to liquor stores to buy the stuff that washes away their pain. I have made it to the bare-bones wine section way in the back of the store, so I'm not especially worried that I'll disturb anyone with this last-stop-before-the-funeral-home collapse.

Lisa, he says again. *Are you OK?*

Not really, I finally say. *I'm about to pick up the ashes.*

Oh.

Dave calmly does his calming-down thing. He is very good at that—comes from experience—and I finally say goodbye. I wander some more. By the time I actually find a bottle of wine, I've recovered my composure. I pay and leave.

I don't know anything about funeral homes. Are they all ramblers that look as though they were built in the early 1960s?

I walk into this one, and there's a reason why somebody

coined the phrase "heavy silence." The silence weighs a ton. A woman greets me.

Is the director in? I ask.

No, he's busy. But I can help you.

I'm here to pick up my father's ashes.

What's the name?

Again, I don't know funeral homes. Aren't they in the sympathy business? She doesn't waste any words on sympathy or kindness. She just disappears and comes back in a few minutes with a tidy ten-inch cube of cardboard. My parents had asked for cardboard. My dad especially had no sentimental bones in his aging body.

The funeral home person hands it to me, and I nearly drop it. Not only does the silence in this place weigh a ton, so does this box of ashes, all that remains of my beloved father.

It's still the middle of the workday in Minnesota, but I make another call from the funeral home parking lot. I shouldn't bother Dave again, so this time I call one of my brothers.

I just picked up the ashes, I tell him.

Oh.

There's that word again.

I forgot about the ashes, he says. *I'm back in the routine at work.*

I fail to process this comment through the slow-cook portion of my brain.

Don't forget about me down here! I gasp.

I'm standing next to my car, the doors are open, and the box of ashes sits on the backseat. Where are you supposed to put ashes? In the front seat because they're important? Or in the backseat because you don't really want to be that close to them? I've never driven around with ashes before. What if I were to get into a car crash? All those movies with funny scenes about ashes? Not funny right now.

And the rest of my brief conversation with my brother is just me feeling flat-out sorry for myself, missing my dad, trying to figure out whether my elderly mother can live without the only partner she's ever had, and staring at a cardboard box containing all that's left of, you know, the beefcake and portrait photographer, the guy I thought I knew so well.

MINNEAPOLIS

A few months after Dad's death, Mom finally agrees to move to the Denver area to be closer to my sister. We are all so relieved that she is no longer twelve hundred miles away from family, a collective sibling sigh wafts back and forth across the plains from Minnesota to Colorado.

By now my mother knows I'm thinking of taking a writerly look at the family oil to try to answer some of the questions that have popped up since Dad died. Why did my grandfather Oscar buy farmland so late in his life? What's the family history with North Dakota's light sweet crude oil? And by the way, how can oil be called light and sweet? I have to look it up. It's light because it has low density and doesn't need much processing to be turned into gasoline. It's sweet because it's low in sulfur. It apparently even tastes and smells a bit sweet. And crude, of course, because the oil hasn't yet been processed.

With my sister's help, Mom packs up those old oil files I saw in Florida and discovers even more files that have gone unexamined for so long they have become one with a closet shelf.

All the years I haven't paid attention to Dad's North Dakota oil? That might have to stop. The fracking frenzy is not just big news around the country; it's big family news. The figures on the oil checks, now arriving in my mother's name, have an unfamiliar string of zeros attached to them.

The box arrives, and it's almost big enough to hold a fridge. Judging by the postage paid, it must hold about thirty pounds of that history.

Some people stand in awe of fine art, a van Gogh sunflower, a Georgia O'Keeffe calla lily. I do, too. But for a writer, there is no finer gift than a fridge-sized box containing mysterious old documents. I set the box smack in the middle of my living room floor, straddle it with my legs, slice through the thick layers of packing tape with a small kitchen knife, and open the top flaps.

Oil lease. It's not that old, dated 2005. In the upper right-hand corner is the Williams County Recorder's seal. In the upper left, it says RETURN TO *so-and-so Petroleum, Inc.* The lease starts this way:

> AGREEMENT, Made and entered into the __ day of January, ____, by and between Walter M. Westberg and Naomi Westberg whose post office address is . . . *blah blah blah* . . . WITNESSETH, That the Lessor, for and in consideration of Ten and more ($10.00+) dollars cash in hand paid . . .

Lessor? What's that? I have to look that up, too. A lessor is the person who conveys property by lease. My parents were the lessors because they owned the mineral rights and they were leasing them to an oil company. But ten bucks? Did this oil company lure my parents into leasing their mineral rights for a measly ten-dollar bonus? Maybe the key words are "and more," emphasized by the plus sign inside the parentheses. I hope so.

And would I really want to sign a lease with an oil company? I think of disasters like the Exxon *Valdez* spill in pristine Alaskan waters and the eighty-seven-day British Petroleum spill in the Gulf of Mexico. Never mind the whole connection between burning fossil fuel, greenhouse gases, and the rapid climate change we're now seeing.

But then there's the money. After my father died and I started telling friends about his North Dakota oil holdings, their immediate reaction was pure open-mouthed delight.

Wow, you're gonna be rich! Wow, are you wealthy yet? Lisa, you dog, you!

My mother holds the rights now, and eventually my siblings and I will inherit—and split—Mom's oil income. In the old days, in Dad's day, that would have been a few thousand dollars per year. A few hundred thousand is more typical these days. I could lounge around all day with a big box of bonbons and decide whether to keep the money, give away the money, or, as I say, keep the money. I now dream about the money and all the things I could do with it.

I've heard there are North Dakota farmers making a million dollars a month. That's not us, but the jump in income has been enough to prompt plenty of family conversations.

Yes, I tend to vote for political candidates with strong environmental positions, and yes, I once organized a bunch of disorganized neighbors to help save a heron rookery from being carved up for development, but as much as anyone I love cheap energy. I love to take airplanes to gorgeous places; wear petroleum-based fleece jackets and zip them up with petroleum-based plastic zippers; drive my car to the grocery store at the last minute because I forgot to buy olives for this recipe; and then eat the olives, processed no doubt with energy provided by fossil fuel.

A newspaper clipping. November 29, 1951, *Fargo Forum*. The headline:

Here's Outline of First Oil Pool to Be Defined in N.D.

It isn't much of an article, mostly just a map of Williams County in western North Dakota with a big amoeba-shaped outline superimposed on the county's grid of sections. Long ago, North Dakota and much of the United States were neatly carved up into square-mile sections. Portrayed this way, the state looks like a sheet of graph paper, the kind my dad wrote letters, notes, everything on. The amoeba shape was presumably the celebrated oil pool, about thirteen miles long by six miles wide. That word "pool" is a misnomer. Oil doesn't form a big underground lake; it occupies the tiny pore spaces in rock, but that would be hard to describe in a headline:

**Here's First Underground Rock Formation
in Which Pore Spaces Are Filled with Oil!**

Oil was discovered in the state in 1951. Someone—was it my grandfather?—inked a small square inside one of the sections with the number 00 and a slightly bigger rectangle inside another section with the number 160. Did he own these rectangles? If so, his parcels were nicely contained within the amoeba oil pool.

You know my grandfather Oscar was hoping somebody would drill for oil on his land.

The *Fargo Forum* newspaper staff had marked the places on the map where oil had already been found and where drilling had resulted in a dry hole. Oscar's two farm parcels were about halfway between a couple of dry holes and a couple of producing wells.

How he and my grandmother Meg must have studied this map. How they must have speculated about their chances for making money. I can picture it: the two of them sitting in their living room in Williston . . . They've just cut the article out of the paper . . . Oscar (probably) gets out a pen and marks the location of his farm parcels on the newsprint map . . .

We could fix the back steps, my grandmother says. *We could wallpaper the upstairs bedroom.*

Don't get your hopes up, says my grandfather. *This North Dakota oil might not amount to anything in our lifetime.*

A 1956 exchange of letters between my grandfather and an oil company executive:

Oscar:

Can you tell us anything about future development on Section 31 and Section 32? We are of course still waiting for drilling by Pure Oil on the three locations they said they would drill.

The oil executive:

At the moment there are no wells being drilled and no locations have been announced . . . Except for bad weather both of the Westberg wells have been producing almost every day. The weather has been extremely bad in this area.

Things in Williston are about the same as always. The new bank is almost complete. Williston won 2nd place in the Western playoff. Senator Carol Day died in a plane crash. This is about all the news.

Kindest regards to you and your family,

Playoffs? An oil company executive was chatting with my grandfather about playoffs? It was March, so it must have been basketball, and it was 1956, so it must have been boys' basketball.

Another 1956 letter from my grandfather, a few months before he died, this time to the president of Cardinal Drilling Co.:

Dear _____,
I remember distinctly when you and your brother had luncheon with us in the old homestead shack. The shack is still there, but we have built considerably in granaries, machine shed, and a 3-bedroom house for our renters . . . You may tentatively tell us what you have in mind with the opportunity of further negotiation as I have not looked into this. I had a light coronary.

He's just had a heart attack, but he's once again chatting up an oil company executive. His tone is not just polite; it's downright obsequious. *You may tentatively tell us what you have in mind.* Don't believe I've ever started a sentence that way.

I want to see that homestead shack. Is it still there? Didn't he farm the land himself? And where exactly is this farm? I have never wondered these things before.

By now, I've grabbed fistfuls of files and moved to a comfy chair. Only toddlers and yoga masters can sit on the floor for a long time without their backs kinking up.

A hand-drawn map of the crops on one of Oscar's farm parcels:

26 acres rye. 20 acres wheat. Prairie. 22 acres fallow. 15 acres safflower. 15 acres barley. Two oil wells.

Two letters in the late 1950s and early '60s from my father to the North Dakota farm manager who was hired shortly after my grandfather died:

If you think the bank balance can stand $200 a piece for us, it would come in handy for Xmas. We leave it up to you.

And a year later . . .

I am once again broke and much interested in some money when you see fit to sell grain, etc.

These words stagger me. By then, my dad was a chemical engineer at 3M. Sure, he had four children, but wasn't an engineer's salary at a multinational corporation enough to support a family? Were his finances so tight he had to ask his farm manager for a $200 advance against grain sales? And where was I? Running around oblivious! Playing hopscotch on the sidewalk or being chased by my fourth-grade boyfriends!

I find that after a mere hour with these documents, I have started to slide off my comfy chair toward the floor again, this time flat on the floor, not sitting. Sometimes I do my best thinking in a prone position, and today, here's what I think:

Oil companies offer cash as an incentive, but this box lures me as effectively as a fistful of cash. It makes me want to abandon the things that usually compete for my time—paying the bills, going to work, visiting our daughters and our friends—to explore my family's history with North Dakota oil and, most of all, to see how I fit into this new world even though I'm not sure I'll like what I discover.

PRIMARY TERM

> It is agreed that this lease shall remain in force for
> a term of ___ years from this date . . .
>
> *This is how long the mineral owner gives the mineral
> developer, the oil company, to develop the property for
> the purpose of producing oil and gas.*

MINNEAPOLIS

Dad had asked that his ashes be scattered somewhere near his hometown of Williston, North Dakota. And he didn't ask his family for much, so we're anxious to grant this one wish. Some of us, within days of his death, start thinking about a family caravan to western North Dakota.

Williston. It's the town where Dad was born and spent most of his childhood. It's on a big bend in the Missouri River just downstream from its confluence with the Yellowstone River, fifteen miles from the Montana border, less than a hundred miles from Saskatchewan. A dusty railroad town and pretty much out of the way, Williston is at the heart of North Dakota's latest oil boom.

A family caravan. It's a great idea. But can my family pull this off? We all love each other, but we generally resist herding up.

Since I'm already laying plans to investigate the family oil, I start writing a note to determine who is interested in the caravan idea and what the best weekend is.

> Hi everyone,
> This summer, we're hoping to honor Grandpa's life by honoring his wishes: drink an Uff-da beer and sprinkle his ashes in western North Dakota.

My note goes on to say that if you need to, you can accomplish this trip in three days: one long day of driving to Williston, one day for ash sprinkling, one long day of driving back to the Twin Cities.

The audience for this heads-up note is sixteen family members:

A brother who is a confirmed homebody and doesn't particularly enjoy traveling anymore;

Another brother and his wife with such frenetic work travel schedules that nobody ever knows where they are. When I call them the first thing I say is, *Hi;* the second thing I say is, *Where are you?* They have two grown daughters, one in the tyrannical grip of pharmacy school, the other with very little vacation time;

My sister and her husband, both retired. That part's good, but their two busy grown-up kids—one in grad school, one a musician—are both on the East Coast, about eighteen hundred miles from western North Dakota;

Uncle Rich, nearly ninety, who has the usual assortment of aches and pains that people in their ninth decade tend to have;

And Dave and I, both of us working, but both of us always eager for road trips and vacations. Our two grown daughters and their spouses are all working and would need to ask for time off.

My mother, a native of Minot, North Dakota, is not on my list. She would love to go, but her knees would probably never forgive ten hours of driving.

All told, we range in age from a few years out of college to well past Social Security eligible. We're single, engaged, married, divorced, widowed. One of us is an immigrant; the rest are natives. We work or have worked in industries ranging from roofing granules to finance, hospitality to health care. Some of us have struggled with unemployment. Some of us have enough money, some of us wish we had more, but all of us worry about it. Everybody has a sense of humor but not the same sense. We don't agree on politics or religion. Some of us have never been to North Dakota. None of us has ever been a farmer, and none of us has ever drilled for oil.

I want everybody to come, but not everybody will, I tell myself. My note goes to my sister first because that's just how I do things. I punch "send."

My sister, who is the most organized person I know and was once hired by a CEO to make his manufacturing operation more efficient, waits about twenty-four hours to send back her suggestions and questions. She might have had to lock herself in the bathroom to show that kind of restraint. Her list of suggestions is substantially longer than my original note.

I sigh. It's not that I *can't* organize my way out of a paper bag. I *can,* but it helps if there isn't too much stuff in the bag. And we probably don't have enough time for me to indulge in my usual habit of asking, *What's the rush?* Or time for me to realize at the last minute the complexities of organizing a family caravan. As my friends (the *Are-you-wealthy-yet?* friends) have pointed out, *There's an oil boom out there! Have you booked a hotel?* they shout. And really, they just about shout. *It's crazy out there!* they add, as though they've been to Williston several times.

I KNOW *there's an oil boom!* I'm tempted to shout back.

Better to cede this organizing task to my sister. But one trip arrangement is clear in my mind. Our dear Uncle Rich should fly to the Twin Cities from his home in Pennsylvania. We could pick him up at the airport, then he could ride with one of us to North Dakota.

Rich and my father, only eleven months apart in age, were raised like twins by their parents, Oscar and Meg. Rich looks and sounds like my father. I find myself calling Rich regularly, comforted by this surviving link to my father and his past, which none of us knows much about.

Do you still want to go to North Dakota this summer? I ask.

Yes! Rich says. *I'm going to drive.*

You are? From Pennsylvania?

Oh, sure. I love to drive.

If my elderly dad had announced the same thing, I would have argued with him. But uncles and nieces have an extra degree of separation between them. Instead of arguing, I sidle around with questions.

How about flying to the Twin Cities? Wouldn't that be faster?

I don't like to fly, he says. *No, I'll drive.*

End of conversation. Is it even legal for a ninety-year-old to drive? I should look that up.

In the hands of my sister, a spreadsheet is born. The only thing I like about it is the name she has assigned to it: *North Dakota or Bust.*

My hostility toward spreadsheets, though, is irrelevant. Over the next few weeks, my siblings, nieces, sons-in-law, and everyone else fills up the cells (are they called cells?) assigned to each weekend of June, July, and August with green *OKs,* yellow *Possiblys,* and red *Nos.* Even I can see that just one weekend is green from top to bottom.

I dig around in the glove compartment of our car for a good map of North Dakota because we'll need a good map. I find maps of Minnesota, the Twin Cities, and Wisconsin, and then a number of nonmap items such as outdated insurance cards, wet wipes, an unidentified piece of ex-food. I check the trunk, the backseat, and the floor of the backseat. I finally find a North Dakota road map in a closet in our apartment amidst a stash of miscellaneous unfiled expense records.

But I soon realize a simple road map isn't going to do it. If we decide to sprinkle my father's ashes at the site of his father's farm, all we have are legal descriptions expressed in section, township, and range, which I barely understand. I'm such a city slicker. If these terms ever applied to Minneapolis, they don't now. These legal descriptions say nothing of practical things like roads.

I call Uncle Rich again.

Do you know where your dad's old farm is? I ask him. *Do you know how to get there from Williston?*

Before he retired, my uncle was an engineer who worked for Bell Laboratories. Bell Labs was the epicenter of research and development in his day, attracting brainy people who later won Nobel Prizes for their work on radio astronomy, the transistor, and lasers. Uncle Rich was valedictorian of his high school class, graduated from the University of North Dakota, and can talk at length about the Higgs boson, but his directions to the farm would never actually get you to the farm.

They go something like this: *You drive north on, I think it's 85, north of Williston for a while, then you head east on—what is it?, I can't remember the number of the road—but you go for a while, not too far, it's north of Tioga, or you could go north from Highway 2, then you turn left on a country road . . . It's near so-and-so's farm. If you see so-and-so's farm, you're right there.*

I order an atlas, the kind of map that shows so much detail, it assigns names to the sloughs and marshes and labels them with little swamp-grass icons. These maps show every twitch in every gravel road. True, they aren't GPS. I don't have GPS. And they aren't the satellite images that the National Security Agency and Google use to do God knows what, but for our purposes, an atlas ought to do it.

For decades, neither the state of North Dakota nor its hotels have attracted much national attention. For the most part, North Dakota has been a quiet rural state with a declining population. There were two earlier oil booms, the first when oil was discovered in 1951 and another when oil prices shot up after the oil embargo in the mid-1970s.

But when someone got the idea of drilling horizontally into the Bakken Shale, setting off explosives and injecting water, chemicals, and sand at high pressures to fracture the oil-bearing rocks, the resulting success sent similar shock waves through North Dakota's hotel industry. In a classic example of supply and demand, the availability and price of hotel rooms in Williston leaped in opposite directions.

One Williston hotel clerk tells me an oil company has booked the whole place for the foreseeable future. Another hotel is $249 a night. Because I plan to stay in the state to do research after the ash-sprinkling, that price would add up to several thousand dollars, not too appealing. Another one is much cheaper, $121 a night, but several customers with marginal spelling abilities have trashed it online:

DUMP.

Nasty [with a string of exclamation points]

Welcome to the Bates Hotel.

It was the most discusting place I have ever stayed at.

The place should be condemmed.

I don't understand how a place like this stays open. Please do not waste your money on this-;motel."

I finally find a reasonably priced hotel with this ringing endorsement from one customer:

First if all avoid Williston at all costs. But if you must vencher into the abyss, this hotel is in my opinion the best place to place your head at night.

Dave floats the idea of renting vans and driving in groups of five, ten, however many the vans hold. But our daughters and their spouses take one sniff of that plan and wrinkle their noses. First, there's the problem of music. If you have the latest mobile device, they argue, you'd be fine. But what if you don't? You'd have to listen to the truly awful music chosen by someone else in the van.

Then there's the problem of sitting butt to butt with family for ten hours through the grinding traffic of the Twin Cities and the miles and miles of countryside, and let's face it, love of family would get you about as far as Fargo, and then you'd want out.

Like live-free-or-die Americans, we all make our own driving, flying, or train-riding plans, and Dave's idea dies a quick death.

In the end, our collective ignorance of family history and geography do not stop us. My sister's spreadsheet, electronic communications, and a collective respect and love for my father are the means by which we herd up this unherdable family for our trip west.

When I should be in bed, I line up my own music. I don't like to rely on being able to pick up a radio signal in remote places, and I can't get the fancy Internet stations in my car, so I have to bring my own tunes, music that might generate a few sparks as it vibrates the air over the northern plains. B. B. King or John Lee Hooker or Londoners like Mark Knopfler.

An old friend suggests a variety of tunes from on-the-road classics like Bruce Springsteen's "Pink Cadillac" to obscure contemporary Swedish music in honor of Oscar and my Swedish roots.

Here's a Swedish murder ballad set to indie or rock, she says with a straight face.

Some of her suggestions seem inspired by love, not logic, like "There Ain't No Grave" by Johnny Cash.

Ain't never been played like this before, she declares.

Good enough for me.

———————————

While our caravan plans evolve, I press ahead with my own mission to flesh out my family's oil history.

If your family had mineral rights in North Dakota, and those rights are now paying in the many thousands rather than the tens and hundreds of dollars, you'd want to learn a little bit about the whole business, right? The checks are coming, but what if one month the check doesn't come?

And maybe you've learned that horizontal drilling has forced some changes. When a horizontal well is drilled, all of the mineral owners within a specified two-square-mile area receive checks if the well produces. But there are so many things you don't know.

You can first ask questions of your elderly mother, the mineral rights holder, but she tells you that she didn't keep track of the oil stuff. *That was your dad!*

You can turn to the state of North Dakota and learn quite a bit. The state has a website with basic data on each well and a great interactive map.

But if you want to know about your family's mineral rights, the state employees tell you in a way that makes you realize they've said these words a million times to a million other bewildered mineral rights holders: you have to go to the county courthouse and check the records.

That's all fine, but what if you're in Minneapolis, at least a ten-hour drive from Williams County? Naturally, you'd think you could call the oil company, the operator of the well, and ask a few questions. That's what you'd think, and that's what I did.

I call one of the companies that sends my mother oil royalties, and the woman who answers the phone is delighted to help me. She doesn't mind giving the information to the daughter of a mineral rights holder, perhaps because the information I am asking for is all contained in public records. Or maybe she's just nice.

Another company stops me right away and says I am not listed as a person who is entitled to receive information about these mineral rights. That makes some sense. It made less sense for me to say, *Well, you see, I'm the mineral rights holder's daughter, and I'm the one writing the book. My mother, the mineral rights holder, is not.* So I don't even bother to say it.

Lesson learned? There are oil companies staffed by people willing to help and oil companies staffed by people who aren't.

As I sit at home, far away from Williston and still trying to solve mineral rights mysteries, I resort to a tactic that, as a University of Minnesota School of Journalism and Mass Communication graduate, sends my blood pressure scooting up.

Deception.

I call a few oil companies and tell them I am the mineral rights holder, my mother. One oil company gives me the information, no problem.

Another company provides me with the information, but the woman I speak with is very reluctant and clearly does not believe me. I'm not sure why. I provided her with the proper owner number. I leave messages with two other companies, and they never call me back. Even resorting to tactics of questionable ethics doesn't always pan out.

A North Dakota state employee acknowledges that it can be frustrating trying to contact the oil companies. He encourages me to check out the public records at the you-know-where.

I also wonder why my father signed a lease in 1957 entitling him to royalties from a 1955 well. You can sign a lease after the well is already pumping?

Never mind the next question that occurs to me: is that lease, signed about sixty years ago—long before computers, long before hydraulic fracturing, and just after the Korean Conflict—is that lease in force today?

It is. I can't believe it.

What you'll wind up doing is what I am tempted to do: give up. Maybe this is too hard. I could just watch my mother's money roll in.

Two truths have already emerged:

1. I don't ever expect to completely understand oil drilling and mineral rights in North Dakota.

2. The oil industry is not just an industry. It's a culture with

a rich lexicon and an intricate set of rules. Question it and you drive north in a southbound lane.

It's a late winter morning, and I'm on my way to work. As a tutor, I help frazzled college students with their papers. We talk about everything from thesis statements to comma splices to the addictive eggrolls at the deli down the hall.

I live in southeast Minneapolis, and the first part of any car trip for me starts with the university district, an area with mind-boggling traffic. We have the usual mix of cars-trucks-buses, and even though it's winter, there's a bicyclist, and there's another one. Then a batch of walkers and runners. And then a skateboarding student going against the traffic in the bike lane. So it goes.

After I get through the commercial district known as Dinkytown, I turn right onto a back road through an industrial area. I feel my alert level start to drop from fire-engine red to normal, maybe orange. I love this part of my commute because I used to take the same route on my bicycle just after college to get back and forth from my studio apartment in St. Paul to Dave's apartment in northeast Minneapolis. I tell my daughters these were our courting days. They find this term hilarious.

I also like the road because, for some reason, I like trains and this road is flanked by railroad tracks. I doubt this fondness has anything to do with my family's association with trains. My maternal grandfather built bridges and trestles for the Soo Line in North Dakota, and my dad and Uncle Rich worked summers on a section gang for the Great Northern Railway.

It's more likely just a visceral thing. I like the rumble and power of the locomotives, and I tend to prefer trains with lots of engines. If there are four engines on a train going west, I figure they're heading over the Rockies, and I wish I were going along. I also like to wonder where the train has been and what's in those cars. I know a few names—tanker car, hopper car—elementary things like that. A friend of mine is a train buff; he knows everything. With me, the affection is more childlike, not much more sophisticated than choo-choo.

Today a train is moving east, a little slower than my car is moving. Usually the locomotives pull a mix of cars, but this train is all tanker cars, all black and bullet shaped and many of them new. I can't see the beginning or end of the string.

When the road comes close to the tracks, I slow down so that I'm going about the same speed. Now I can read the number on the red placard with flames on it: 1267. I have to look it up later. Petroleum crude. Is there North Dakota oil inside these railcars? *This could be my family's oil!* Is the oil boom showing up right here in my neighborhood?

Number 1267 on the flammable materials placard identifies the contents of this tanker car as petroleum crude oil. Lisa Westberg Peters

GRANTSBURG, WISCONSIN

I'm a Minnesotan. I know it's smart to bolt outside as soon as the weather warms up in the spring. Even if the previous winter didn't keep you locked inside for months, the next winter probably will.

Using this logic, my daughter and I grab the first nice day in the spring and drive north for a hike led by a naturalist near the St. Croix River, the river of my childhood where I spent whole summers with either a canoe paddle or a book in my hands.

We walk into the visitor center and a half dozen heads—all gray haired—turn our way. Lord! Why is it only old people (plus my daughter, and what's wrong with her?) are interested in wildflower hikes?

We spend the next hour and a half at flower height and within earshot of the river. It feels like an hour and a half well spent.

On the way back to the visitor center, our guide casually mentions that a new mining operation has opened up nearby.

They're mining frac sand, she says.

Oh, yeah? I say.

I knew about the recent surge in midwestern frac sand mining, but I had thought the mines were all south or east of here. Somewhere else. Somewhere far away. And now she was saying that the fracking frenzy was right here, a few hundred feet from the St. Croix.

Yeah, she says, *but I haven't heard about any problems.*

Lots of trucks, I suppose.

Well, she laughs, *if there are, it would be Minnesota's problem.*

The St. Croix serves as the border between Minnesota and Wisconsin on this stretch of its course. Our guide says the company plans to truck the sand across the river to a processing plant about thirty miles west in a small Minnesota town called North Branch.

So. There's a frac sand mine next to the St. Croix, my river.

A few days later, my newspaper tells me that the new frac sand mine near Grantsburg accidentally dumped a thick goop of sand and water into the pristine St. Croix for five days before a hiker finally noticed it and photographed it.

Even as our guide was expressing optimism about the Grantsburg sand mine, the mine operator was busy repairing the berm that had failed.

It's sixty-nine degrees and brilliantly sunny, a great day for a trip to a frac sand mine. Whenever I drive north in Minnesota, I watch for hawks perched on the light standards or eagles circling overhead. This time, all I'm thinking about is sand.

I'm a sand collector. I like the feel of sand, the variety in colors, and especially the beautiful places—the beaches, volcanoes, cliffs, and islands—where I collect it. Today I want to collect sand from a frac sand mine.

I examine the trucks heading north and south. What is that truck hauling? Or this one? Would they haul frac sand across the country in dump trucks? I doubt it, but I don't really know. What would a long-haul sand truck look like?

Just after I cross the St. Croix River into Wisconsin on Highway 70, I see a turnoff to a St. Croix National Scenic Riverway site called the Sandrock Cliffs. I'll bet a million bucks those cliffs are made of the same sand that everybody—from international conglomerates to anyone with a backhoe—wants these days. I'll bet it's the same sand the oil industry is using to keep open the tiny fractures in the shale as escape routes for oil and gas.

I turn off the highway onto a series of smaller and smaller roads that eventually turn to gravel. From a parking lot at the end of the road, it's a short hike to the river.

In its brochure about the Sandrock Cliffs, the National Park Service encourages visitors to *discover clean water, lush landscapes, and quiet solitude along the St. Croix National Scenic Riverway, a national park that with your help protects 252 miles of wild and scenic river corridor.*

Today, standing on the sandstone cliffs above this federally protected river, it's two out of three: clean water and lush landscapes. Quiet solitude? Not so much. I can hear the hum of mining machinery. I haven't seen the mine, but now I know it's very close.

A young man comes to the nearby river landing to let his dog splash in the water. He says if I take the high trail through the woods, I will be able to look down through the trees and see the mine. I try, but an enormous pile of brush—storm debris from a recent blowdown—blocks the trail.

I get back in the car. There just has to be a road somewhere for dump trucks to arrive empty and leave full of sand. I start driving back east on Highway 70, and that's when I see a gravel road to the right marked "Dead End." Bingo. I turn onto it and drive for about a mile through thick forest before the sand mine, in all its humming-machine glory, opens up in front of me. I stop the car a few hundred feet from the gate.

Now that I've found the mine, it suddenly dawns on me that the guys running the mine might not exactly welcome me, a curious writer and sand collector with a camera and a baggie. I'm not even sure this road is public, but I haven't seen any signs saying it's private.

I start taking photos anyway, but when a giant red pickup leaves the mine and approaches my car, I stop. All of a sudden, pointed questions and brisk declarative sentences start to form in my head: *Screw the book research! Wouldn't it be more fun to write a romance novel or a puff piece about the Grantsburg Chamber of Commerce? I'm too old for this kind of excitement!*

The driver, a young man, stays in the cab of his truck and asks if he can help me.

No, no, I assure him. *I'm leaving.*

Were you taking photos? he asks. Odd how the question makes you feel as though you're doing something illegal.

Yes, I say. *Just curious about the mine* [it's true!], *and I'm leaving* [also true!].

I drive away feeling like a criminal, without a good over-head photo of the mine and without a sample of that beautiful buff-colored sand.

Time to go home. I drove 165 miles today and got thirty-three miles per gallon, which means I used five gallons of gasoline trying to photograph a mine that produces sand for the process of oil drilling, which produces petroleum crude, which is used to produce gasoline.

Dave works as a journalist in the Twin Cities, but hidden inside him is a modern-day Meriwether Lewis. He would have fit right in with the Corps of Discovery, keeping an eye out for bears and recording his findings in journals. When he hears about my frac sand frustrations, he goads me into trying again. His attitude at times like this is, *What are you saving yourself for?*

We return to hike a loop trail that begins near Highway 70. *It's just a mile to the mine,* I say. *I know we'll see it; I just know it.*

And we do, but not until we hike over, around, and under dozens of blown-down trees. There are still a few upright trees in the St. Croix National Scenic Riverway, but today it looks like a horizontal forest.

We finally reach a spot on a ridge where we can get a great view of the mine through the trees. I climb onto a fallen tree to snap several photos of a cluster of enormous cream-colored sand cones surrounded by dark green forest, and then I suggest we get out of there. I'm not even going to try to approach the mine again to snatch a sample of sand.

But we apparently aren't finished with the obstacle course otherwise known as the Sandrock Cliffs Trail. The return loop of the trail runs closer to the river, and because of all the rain and high water levels, part of it is underwater. We start slogging through black, stagnant muck. It's mid-calf, and we can't tell if the ground beneath the muck is level, and we sure can't see the trail. I manage to enhance the experience with such helpful observations as:

This is horrible!

Oh my God, I can't believe this.

Worms! Did you see the worms?

The deep-sea diving portion of the path is a mess. It's also about a hundred, maybe a hundred and fifty feet long, as far as the bustling new industrial operation is from a national park.

I may be wobbly with all my fence-sitting, but society isn't giving me a lot of time to dig into my family's history with oil and come up with an answer to my dilemma. Mile-long trains are carrying North Dakota oil through my neighborhood, and frac sand mines are opening up on the banks of my childhood river. Nobody is waiting for me.

Frac sand mine in Grantsburg, Wisconsin, located next to a national park, the St. Croix National Scenic Riverway. Lisa Westberg Peters

GRANTING CLAUSE

> . . . all that certain tract of land situated in the County of Williams, State of North Dakota described as follows, to-wit: Township ____, Range _____, Section _____

> *The property named is the property the mineral developer plans to explore and develop.*

DRIVING WEST FROM MINNEAPOLIS
TO WILLISTON, NORTH DAKOTA

I'm opposed to getting up before six in the morning. Coffee doesn't confer its usual I-can-conquer-the-world feeling. It just adds an annoying buzz to the bleariness. But the car is packed, and I feel ready. For this trip, I want to do several things: fulfill my father's wish to have his ashes sprinkled in his home state, see the drilling frenzy, poke into my family's history with oil, bag up some frac sand, chat with North Dakotans about the oil boom, and photograph an oil train speeding across the plains.

And, of course, I hope to answer this question: how do I, an environmentalist, fit into the booming North Dakota oil world? I've decided the best way to answer that question is to ask more questions. For this trip, I want to see and learn as much as possible.

I put Dad's ashes in the trunk of our car several days ago so that I would stop having nightmares about forgetting them. Imagine participating in a family caravan from Minneapolis to Williston, North Dakota—that's six hundred miles or so—to sprinkle ashes and then having no ashes to sprinkle.

We drive past two central Minnesota power plants, the nuclear power plant at Monticello and the coal-fired power plant at the town of Becker, both operated by Xcel Energy.

Industrial-strength transmission lines follow the freeway for miles, but as heavy duty as they seem, they clearly have room on their arms for more lines and more juice.

This morning, our daughters and their husbands got an earlier start than us, which just has to be a violation of the laws of nature. We get this road trip advice from them at 5:26: *Don't stop at the McDonald's in Monticello. They're slow.*

One brother is driving with Uncle Rich, thank God, and they're leaving the Twin Cities later than we are. My sister-in-law and her two daughters are boarding the train from St. Paul's Amtrak station and are leaving late tonight. My sister's family flew to the Twin Cities from Denver, and my other brother is riding with them. They should be on the road by now.

That's fifteen, a great turnout for this destination funeral.

My pulse still quickens when I head west even though I've driven west from the Twin Cities on so many routes and so many occasions. I love to see the face of the continent change from rolling hills and lakes to arid plains to mountains and snow. As soon as we cross the state line into North Dakota I expect to jot these adjectives in my notebook: *Flat, dry, hot, sunny, windy.*

As we drive through the heart of central Minnesota, we can see a thunderstorm heading toward us on the western horizon. The temperature drops five degrees, and the rain falls in sheets. I draw a picture of the clouds and the curved ribbons of rain after the center of the storm passes us by.

Maybe the rain is falling in Morris, which is close to where my grandfather was born to Swedish immigrant farmers more than a hundred and twenty years ago on land very recently occupied by the Dakota people. He left his childhood home later on for North Dakota. I do know that much about him.

When I was young, my mother told me I needed to read Ole Rølvaag's book *Giants in the Earth* in order to understand my people. In college, I finally read about the gut-wrenching struggles of Scandinavian immigrants who set out for Dakota Territory. The story begins innocently enough:

> Bright, clear sky over a plain so wide that the rim of the heavens cut down on it around the entire horizon . . . Bright, clear sky to-day, to-morrow, and for all time to come.
> . . . And sun! And still more sun!

It's spring, but you can guess it gradually comes round to winter. I dare anyone to write a better snowstorm scene than Ole Rølvaag. The main character, Per, and his fellow settlers are traveling across the prairie in early winter with their oxen and sleighs, a storm starts to brew, and they devise a means to stay together.

> "This is what we must do," said Hans Olsa: "We'll pass a rope from sleigh to sleigh, so that we won't lose each other in the storm. Isn't that right, Per Hansa?"

But it's like the old tales when the hero or heroine is told not to open the box. You know they're going to open the box, and in *Giants in the Earth,* you know something bad will go wrong with the rope plan, and sure enough, at Per's expense, it does:

> A violent jerk came on his rope, so strong that he almost plunged forward. To save himself from being dragged off his sleigh he was forced to let go his hold.

Already he's cut loose, and that's just the beginning of the storm. The scene goes on for eight pages—eight! By the end, you're gasping for breath.

One hundred and fifty years after Per lost the rope, our summer caravan of travelers across the plains is held together by the modern-day ropes of cell phones and interstate freeway.

When we finally cross the Red River of the North, the state line at Moorhead and Fargo, I find my list of adjectives to be nearly worthless. I should have remembered—the eastern part of North Dakota is wetter than the western, and today it is:

Not hot—it's about sixty degrees, twenty degrees colder than I expected and forty degrees cooler than it was in Minneapolis earlier this week.

Not flat—there are rolling hills. This beauty throws me off. I had decided that if the oil boom was confined to an ugly, desolate state, maybe that's not so bad.

Not dry—it's blindingly green.

Not windy—perfectly calm.

And today, North Dakotans—at least the ones at the gas station and the visitor center in Fargo—don't swagger like roustabouts or wildcatters. They sound and look so much like me, it's spooky. No strange accent, no unfamiliar mannerisms. I may as well be at home.

PINGREE, NORTH DAKOTA

The first train we see, outside the tiny town of Pingree, is not an oil train. The shiny red locomotive says RRV&W, and I have no idea what that means. Later I learn this is the Red River Valley & Western, a regional railroad. I can't tell what the train is hauling.

Just east of Drake, we finally see our first oil train. Unfortunately, it's stone-cold stopped. And judging by the hollow sound when we thump the tanker cars, the damn thing is empty. Here we are, not just in North Dakota but getting closer and closer to the oil fields, and all I get is a photo of an empty, stopped oil train.

Oil train parked near Drake, North Dakota, about a hundred fifty miles east of the Bakken oil patch. Lisa Westberg Peters

MINOT, NORTH DAKOTA

In Minot, on U.S. Highway 2, we see our first oil-related billboard. It says:

> *Oil field housing*
> *We know the drill*

Cute.

At Palermo, about fifty miles west of Minot, we finally see our first North Dakota oil well. I lean out the window for photos. In the middle of a field, the pumpjack pumps away, a bright orange flare of natural gas burning nearby. I don't understand the flaring, but I've heard it has something to do with a lack of pipelines.

The oil patch truck traffic picks up near Stanley, and here's

North Dakota pumpjack brings up oil, natural gas, and fluids from two miles beneath the surface. The natural gas is flared off. Lisa Westberg Peters

where I start to feel vulnerable in our little red car with its beach ball profile (easy to spot in parking lots, not that useful on the freeway). I don't know what half the trucks are for. Some look like they'd hold water or liquids and others resemble—strange as it sounds—silver cows' udders. Gravity must help unload whatever is in those trucks, and it's probably not milk. Then there's a red truck, a thicket of pipes and instruments on wheels. Not sure what that's for, either.

Some trucks are hauling big boxy things that must be portable homes. Maybe those trucks are headed for the notorious man camps where oil workers mix in a fervid stew of testosterone and petrochemicals. The news accounts are gaga over the man camps. Man camps, man camps, man camps!

But North Dakota has seen something resembling this before.

Crowds of strangers—oil operators and scouts, promoters, geologists, drillers, lease buyers and brokers, as well as un-skilled labor—invaded the oil region. The newcomers turned granaries, sheds, and garages into living and business quarters. They and their families jammed community services, crowded schools, wore out roads, and brought on a boom which meant dozens of new enterprises, ranging from lunch counters to oil-field equipment houses.

That was historian Elwyn Robinson's description of North Dakota's first oil boom just after oil was discovered in 1951. There was a second boom in the late 1970s and early '80s. Today's boom is far bigger than either, to be sure, but Robinson goes on to say that in the 1950s, *gas flares lit up the night.* Oil drillers find natural gas along with the oil; they can haul away the oil in trucks, but it isn't that easy with natural gas.

We pass oil well after oil well, pumpjacks nodding up and down, gas flares hissing. Pennsylvanians are pulling up natural gas to be burned in power plants and stoves, and North Dakotans continue to flare it off.

And once again, I record in my notebook the opposite of what I expected: *The countryside is still very green. Canola fields, brilliant yellow, but everything else is green.* And as we continue along on Highway 2, Prairie Public Radio plays the blues. Geez, I didn't even need to bring B. B. King.

WILLISTON, NORTH DAKOTA

Two strikes in the expectations department. One more and I'll be out.

We approach Williston from the north on Highway 2 late in the afternoon and finally pull into our motel's parking lot. We lift suitcases and backpacks out of the trunk, leave the food wrappers and empty water bottles for now, stumble past the sign asking us to clean off our muddy boots, and walk into the lobby.

Late afternoon sun lights up highway signs and storm clouds north of Williston, North Dakota. Lisa Westberg Peters

It'll be about a half hour before you can get into your room, the clerk informs us.

We stare, stupefied.

We had about thirty checkouts today, she explains.

I wouldn't have guessed they had thirty rooms in this place.

The cleaning crew is way behind, she adds, probably because we're still staring. Imagine how much front desk people must hate tired tourists.

We plop into the lobby chairs and wait. And wait. People come and go. Some of them look regular, and some of them look seriously big and overmuscled. I sink deeper into my chair to watch, wondering what this town is like now that the oil industry has seized it by the throat.

I've been in Williston before, but the most recent occasion was a few decades ago. On one of our trips across the West,

Dave and I had lunch at the Plainsman Hotel, iconic Williston landmark.

And when I was a baby, my family visited Grandma Meg and Grandpa Oscar in Williston. By the early 1950s, Oscar was a big man on campus, eager and proud to show off his new granddaughter to his friends. These men might have been some of the same men in the state historical society's photo I found a few nights before my father died. During lunch, my mother tells me, I started throwing food from my high chair.

Finally our room is ready. We hoist our bags and maps and laptop onto our shoulders, trudge down the hall, and open the door to our room. On this short journey from lobby to room, we come to realize why the rates here are relatively low.

I should preface these remarks by saying I'm reluctant to judge North Dakotans harshly; their civilization has been taken over by aliens. On the other hand, they sent out plenty of welcome signals and are now making front-end-loader scoopfuls of money off them. Whoever is running this hotel, with its full occupancy and Manhattan rates, might consider skimming a few bucks off the profit to:

Clean the long trail of slime on the hallway carpet;

Replace the broken radio in our room;

Fix the bathroom door, which has swelled and no longer closes;

Fix the hair dryer's wall mount so that the hair dryer no longer falls off the wall;

Do something—*something*—so that the key card opens the door the first or second time you swipe it, not the eighth or ninth time.

If you stand for twenty minutes alongside U.S. Highway 2 as it passes through Williston, you'll see and hear evidence of the dramatic increase in oil production: water tankers haul millions of gallons pulled from the Missouri River to near- and far-flung hydraulic fracturing jobs; flatbed trucks carry pyramids of pipe and dump trucks haul dirt; those strange

Trucker hauls water for hydraulic fracturing from the Missouri River through Williston to a Bakken well site. Lisa Westberg Peters

Stack of pipes, or well casing, probably destined for a new horizontal well in the Bakken Shale. Lisa Westberg Peters

red trucks bristle with pipes and valves; and the silver udder trucks carry frac sand (I discover after I ask). The stream of truck traffic beats up the roads and kicks up plenty of dust, which settles onto the speed limit signs.

You probably won't see evidence of the dramatic increase in many other things: employment rates and personal income (the good news), and rent, prostitution, human trafficking, and drug trafficking (the bad news). All of these things are booming along with oil production.

If you stand alongside U.S. Highway 85 south of Williston (and by the way, I don't actually recommend that), you'll see how the oil patch is creeping closer and closer to roadless grasslands and badlands where prairie coneflowers and prairie dogs rule. Dave and I have given money to land trusts to protect such places, but conservation efforts in western North Dakota must certainly be dwarfed by the millions devoted to oil development.

We're not tiptoeing around in our search for oil; we're stomping with size-thirteen work boots.

Williston sits near the Missouri River, although a busy set of railroad tracks effectively separates the town from the river. This bluff country is harsh; it's also strikingly beautiful.

Intrepid explorer Meriwether Lewis, busy as he was trying to survive his 3,700-mile journey across the trackless northwest in the early 1800s, focused on the harshness from his campsite:

> The wind blew So hard this morning from N. W. that we dared not to venture our canoes on the river.—

and the winter-ready wildlife:

> The beaver of this part of the Missouri are larger, fatter, more abundant and better clad with fur than those of any other part of the country that I have yet seen; I have remarked also that their fur is much darker.—

It was easier for me, a twenty-first-century traveler, to fall in love with the North Dakota landscape on this particular summer day. The prairie potholes across the state were full of water. The wheat was green and healthy.

And yet I heard a state official talk on Prairie Public Radio about his conversations with the Norwegians over oil. To paraphrase, *They can teach us a lot,* he said. *Their situation is different, of course. They have beautiful mountain scenery that they need to protect. All we have is rolling plains.*

Is he saying it's all right to go full-bore oil drilling because North Dakota is not that cool a place? And isn't that what I thought?

It's true what they say about Williston: this place is wacky. The sense of being among my own people isn't as strong here. This town is on a mission, and the mission is foreign to me.

I still don't get how I, city-girl environmentalist, fit into this remote rural countryside now populated by oil workers, pumpjacks, and gas flares. What brought my family here in the first place? My grandfather Oscar was born in Minnesota. Why did he leave good farmland and the embrace of home and family?

These questions expand the territory I want to explore and launch me on a journey back and forth across the Upper Midwest, from a river town in eastern Iowa to a branch of the old oxcart trail in western Minnesota, from a dining room in Williston to an A-frame cabin on a Wisconsin river.

Don't worry. We'll rejoin the funeral caravan in western North Dakota. But for now, if you'll indulge me, I'm going to let go of the ropes.

IMPLIED COVENANTS

> . . . implied covenants are those which are inferred
> by the law from certain words in a deed which im-
> ply (though they do not express) them.
>
> A LAW DICTIONARY, SECOND EDITION
>
> *The mineral owner assumes the mineral developer,*
> *the oil company, will do certain things simply because*
> *it's an oil company: it will explore for minerals; it will*
> *maintain its equipment; it will market the product.*
> *Those promises go unstated in the contract.*

MCGREGOR, IOWA

I have my feet up, resting from what is bound to become my
new research routine: pull into a hotel parking lot; sling a laptop case and a camera case over one shoulder, a heavy bag
filled with files over the other; drag a suitcase out of my car's
trunk; and then haul my sorry ass into the hotel lobby to register for the night.

Nobody drills for oil in this scenic river town on the Mississippi. I'm not in Clayton County, Iowa, for the oil. I'm here
because this is where Oscar's father, just seven years old at
the time, and Oscar's grandparents first landed after they emigrated from Sweden in 1869.

Iowa was not my clan's final destination. They knew they
wanted to go to Minnesota. But they were doing what so many
Scandinavian immigrants did: they settled temporarily, got
their bearings, and learned some English. They probably hired
themselves out as laborers or domestic servants to earn a little money for supplies and tools, and then they moved on to
where they hoped to find free land. By 1869, there certainly
wasn't much left in northeastern Iowa.

I'm discovering that each research jaunt across the Midwest requires a prejaunt, and it usually begins with Uncle Rich.

Why did our Westberg ancestors leave Sweden? I ask him.

No idea, he says.

Do you know what they did in Sweden?

Nobody ever talked about any of that, he says.

These answers make me crazy and send me to historical society libraries and websites. I finally learn that Oscar's grandparents were named Johannes Jonsson and Ingeborg—let's hope she shortened it to Inge—Ersdotter. They and their four children lived on a farm in the southwestern part of Sweden. I like to think Johannes had rugged Nordic looks and Inge was a Swedish beauty like Ingrid Bergman. I am allowed to think whatever I want because I have no photos of them. Maybe they met at church in Skog, Sweden, and that's where they would have married. The guests would have arrived by horse and buggy or even by foot if they were farm neighbors.

And the children would have immediately followed. No birth control back then.

One tiny entry on a database pops out for me. Johannes didn't list his profession as farmer. He listed it as *ägare*, the Swedish word for owner or proprietor. He must have been a landowner, not a renter or a common laborer. Maybe he was the eldest son and had inherited his father's farm.

His declaration showed pride. Was he ambitious and curious about opportunities in the new world they all knew as Nord Amerika?

The six Jonssons emigrated in a year notorious for one thing: crop failures. Thousands of Swedes had faced a two-year drought, crop failures, and starvation. I am starting to glimpse the reason they left home.

I don't know hunger. Sure, I've felt hungry on occasion, and I've even announced I was starving, but it's the kind of thing you say when the Thanksgiving turkey is taking longer than expected and everybody stands around yakking about it.

Hunger—same word, different order of magnitude— probably drove my people to uproot their lives, board a sailing ship, and cross the Atlantic Ocean toward the unknown. I have trouble imagining that kind of hunger, especially for my own people, even though hunger is not a dusty, historical concept.

The East African immigrants who live in the high-rises across the Mississippi River from me are not far removed from the drought, warfare, and hunger so famously portrayed in news photographs. And news reports today remind me that the global effort to replace high-polluting fossil fuel with corn-based biofuels produces some unintended consequences: hunger for people who rely on cheap corn for food.

Johannes may have had special status as a Swedish landowner, but even special people couldn't make a small stony farm, crop failures, and hunger add up to a fun life.

Hunger almost certainly pushed my people out of Sweden, but something else pulled them to the Midwest.

Around the time the Jonssons were packing up their America chest, a land agent in St. Paul wrote a pamphlet called *Minnesota: Its Advantages to Settlers 1868.* The title was a little vague, but he left nothing to the imagination in his subtitle: *Being a Brief Synopsis of Its History and Progress, Climate, Soil, Agricultural and Manufacturing Facilities, Commercial Capacities, and Social Status; Its Lakes, Rivers, and Railroads; Homestead and Exemption Laws; Embracing a Concise Treatise on Its Climatology, in a Hygienic and Sanitary Point of View; Its Unparalleled Salubrity, Growth and Productiveness, As Compared with the Older States; and the Elements of Its Future Greatness and Prosperity.*

You wouldn't even have to read the book.

This land agent had a particular challenge: less than ten years earlier, a group of Dakota warriors, pushed to starvation by broken treaties, had swept across western Minnesota, killing hundreds of white settlers and destroying farmsteads.

The countryside was emptied, and most tribal members were thrown in prison or banished to reservations farther west.

Now the land was once again being offered to new immigrants.

This land agent told potential settlers that the geographical position of Minnesota was the most favored on the continent, and the products of agriculture attained their most perfect development here. As for the climate, he was emphatic: it was one of the healthiest in the world. Diseases couldn't catch hold in Minnesota because the climate was so damn healthy. Consumption, diarrhea, diphtheria—barely there! And in an outright lie, he claimed that the *dreadful scourge of the human family, the cholera, is . . . unknown here.*

My people may have been able to resist this cocky American promoter's claims. I suspect they were less able to resist the assurances of a fellow Swede who became a land agent for one of Minnesota's fledgling railway companies. He cautioned that the poor settler should not expect to be *released from trouble, toil and privation* in Minnesota. But he did claim that Scandinavians would find this northern state more to their liking than one of the southern states. Sure, the winters were hard, but *the northern dweller thrives best in the north.*

Immigration boosters were everywhere. They worked for the states, the railroads, the U.S. government, or the banks, or they were enterprising capitalists and worked on their own. The message from all of these promoters? *You come over, you're gonna be happy. The fish are jumpin'.*

That promise must have sounded very good to hungry Swedes, even if they knew about the Dakota War.

————————

Imagine how Oscar's grandparents presented the emigration journey to their children in the evenings before their departure. *We're going to take a sailing ship—a big adventure! We'll go to a land where the wheat grows higher than you! You won't ever be hungry again.*

Parents make promises to their children; Dave and I certainly did. There are the everyday promises: *if you behave in the grocery store, sweetie—no tantrums, no running off—I'll buy you a treat at the checkout counter.* And then there are the big honkin' promises: *if you want to go to college, we'll do everything we can to pay for it. And don't be getting any goofy ideas about spending five, six years at college.*

Parents hardly ever write these promises down, but I have always felt that an unwritten promise is just as big a deal as a written promise. Of course, a lawyer might disagree.

But what about the unwritten, typically unuttered Mother of All Promises that most parents and grandparents make, the promise that we will leave a better world for our children and grandchildren? Here's when I start hoping that my lifelong habit of swilling natural resources like cheap wine isn't just a binge for which my descendants will pay. Like a drunk, I glance furtively from side to side when I read about global pollution and the prospect of rising seas, stronger storms, and weather extremes.

Ten years before my people showed up in Nord Amerika, an American named Edwin L. Drake was the first person in the world to deliberately drill for oil. He drilled sixty-nine feet and struck oil near Titusville, Pennsylvania, starting the modern petroleum industry, but that juggernaut didn't build for a while. My people certainly didn't benefit from it. They relied on the wind to get across the Atlantic, and it took them five weeks.

In one of those quirks of research serendipity, I discover there's a sand mine several miles south of McGregor.

The mine's operators dig into the massive sandstone river bluffs, close to the valley where my people first settled and the area known as Swede Ridge, named for the hordes of Scandinavian immigrants streaming here in the 1800s. The mine used to ship the sand out to glass factories, and it was also used in the area for a variety of industrial and commercial purposes. Today the mine ships out—you guessed it—frac sand.

I want to see how busy the mine is, so I head down there from my hotel first thing in the morning and park on the shoulder of Clayton County Road X56. The two-lane road runs parallel to the river along the flat bluff tops. All around me are farm fields, and just ahead is a blacktop road heading downhill through a break in the bluffs. A short way down the hill is a guard shack marking the entrance to the mining company's property. The road serves double duty as entrance to the sand mine and to a grain shipping operation. I'm not going to try to get closer—I can still picture that big red pickup—but I do want to see how many trucks come and go.

Here we go. At 9:14 AM, a semi climbs the hill and turns north on X56. The county road looks as though it should be a sleepy one, but it's not. Semis zoom past regularly in both directions. To take a picture of the sand mining company's sign, I have to run to the middle of the road, snap a photo, and run back to the shoulder.

Because I have post-traumatic stress from my earlier frac sand mine expedition, I half expect somebody to pull over and ask me, *What do you think you're doing? Are you taking pictures?* I called the company this morning to see if the mine offered tours, but a human being didn't answer the phone, and I was quite sure no one would call me back if I left a message.

9:17. Another truck. This one approaches from the north, turns onto the blacktop road, and heads down the hill. This truck looks like a silver caterpillar, a tubelike container with ribs marking the sections.

9:20. Two more trucks leave the mine; one is covered, one is open. Both head north on X56.

9:22. A truck approaches from the south and turns in.

9:26. A truck approaches from the north and turns in. This is a very busy place.

9:30. A truck approaches from the north and turns in.

9:35. A truck climbs the hill and the driver gets out (crap, now they're going to yell at me), but he's just checking something on his truck, and now he's driving away. I've seen eight trucks coming or going from this road in about twenty minutes. That's a truck every three or four minutes. Some of them are probably hauling grain, some are hauling sand, and some are empty. I'm told the sand mine is open twenty-four hours a day, seven days a week. That's some serious commerce.

News stories about the mine say that the owners are hauling frac sand across the river by truck to Wisconsin rail lines and then shipping it to all of the major North American shale plays. North Dakota is one of them. So if you think about it, and I just did, Clayton County, Iowa, a world-class scenic spot on the Upper Mississippi River, is once again a starting point for a steady stream of travelers. In the 1800s, it was hope-filled immigrants; today it's sand-filled railcars.

––––––––––––

I meet Bob, a charming man and a descendant of Clayton County homesteaders. I tell him that my people left the bluffs and valleys of eastern Iowa to homestead in western Minnesota.

How do you think they traveled? I ask. *If you were poor, how would you get there?*

Bob talks about the railroads, which were starting to stitch together the surrounding countryside with track, and the steamships, which were plying the Mississippi. But trains and boats required money, and I figure my people had none.

My guess is they went by horse and buggy, he says.

Or oxcart or a wagon pulled by some kind of beast of burden.

An early plat map of Clayton County shows a wagon trail in this valley. Later it became U.S. Highway 52, passing through Rochester, Minnesota (Mayo Clinic-ville) on its way to St. Paul. It's the route I took to get to McGregor and the route I'll take when I go back to the Twin Cities.

How long do you think it took them to get to St. Paul?

Bob isn't sure, but I think I can figure it out. It's almost two hundred miles to St. Paul. Hard to know exactly how fast oxen traveled, but I'm guessing it was very slowly, maybe three miles per hour or even less. Let's say three. That's sixty-six hours, but remember, the Jonssons had a couple of small children in addition to the teenagers. Let's say they pushed it and traveled ten hours each day. They'd need almost seven days for the trip from McGregor to St. Paul.

On my own return trip to the Twin Cities, I drive a car, so of course, I have to stop for gas. One thing will never be the same for me. Whenever I fill up my car with gasoline, I now wonder if it was refined from North Dakota crude, perhaps even crude pumped from my own family's oil wells.

I miss a turn because this crazy trail-turned-highway zigs or zags at each small town, and then I stop to take a photo of a very modern wind turbine standing guard over this old wagon route.

Mindful of the nineteenth-century travelers, I try to appreciate how comfortable my car is—the cushy seat, the suspension system not yet beaten up by a steady diet of potholes in Minneapolis. And for miles, I listen to a Decorah radio station, which brags that it's on the vanguard of contemporary music. Decorah is home to Luther College, a magnet for Scandinavian American Lutherans. I'm grateful today for the Lutherans. They not only believe in God; they also believe in strong radio signals.

The drive should have taken me three and a half hours, but because I dawdled a bit, it takes me four.

Oscar's grandparents left no written record of their emigration from Sweden to the Midwest. No vivid tales of the blinding midwestern snowstorms and the jumpin' fish. No written wisdom for descendants to learn from. My first reaction to this fact is: *Would it have killed them to keep a journal and tuck it under the floorboards for later discovery by somebody like me?* But when I take a closer look at the 1870 census from Clayton County, Iowa, I see that Johannes and Inge could read but not write. My people were illiterate.

STEVENS COUNTY, MINNESOTA

To get to the Westberg clan's Minnesota homestead—my grandfather Oscar's birthplace—I head northwest from Minneapolis on another modern road that follows old wagon trail routes. I peel off at Sauk Centre to head due west.

When I cross into Pope County, the sign announcing this fact jogs my memory. This county was the scene of a noisy ruckus in the late 1970s when two power utilities proposed a high-tension power line through the countryside and some of the local residents came unglued, claiming the line would threaten their health. They protested with vigor and imagination.

One group of farmers set up a manure spreader and sprayed themselves with manure so that Minnesota state troopers would have to think twice before forcibly removing them from the scene.

As a reporter for the *St. Cloud Daily Times,* Dave helped cover the story. From his editor's point of view, it was totally great stuff. You've got your visuals, your angry quotes, your high drama, and your smelly cow shit—a bonus. Things didn't turn out well for the protesting farmers; the transmission line went through.

Just west of the epicenter of the power line protest is Oscar's home turf. Farm country. Rolling plains, a few groves of trees, a few lakes. I hadn't expected to see so many irrigation rigs, but these days, more and more Minnesota farmers are drilling wells and pumping groundwater, a practice that is starting to worry hydrologists. The farmers do it to boost their yields, of course, and no doubt their profits.

When the immigrants left Iowa, they came here, filed a claim, and built a log house. There was no oil here, either, just great farmland.

My grandfather was born in the log house, and I have a photo of him standing next to it. He is probably in his sixties, but his posture is erect and formal. He wears a suit and tie, he holds a fedora in his hand, and a small, unidentified boy stands next to him.

Compared to my well-dressed grandfather, his birthplace looks unkempt, except for the roof, which is clearly not the original. There's a tree behind the house, but otherwise the shack stands alone on the plains.

My first reaction is disbelief. How could anyone be born in so small, so remote, so primitive a structure? I was born in

My grandfather, Oscar Westberg, visits his family's homestead shack in Stevens County, Minnesota, where he was born. Family photo

a hospital. My daughters were born in hospitals. Everyone I know was born in a hospital.

The farmer who lives on the Westberg homestead land today has welcomed my visit. T. J. is seventy-eight and retired from farming but still working. He drives a semi around the Midwest, delivering grain to elevators. When I talked to him, it was late in the evening and he was driving and speaking on a cell phone. This guy must be one of those old Norwegians made of steel or lutefisk or something.

I turn off the state highway onto County Road 1 around three in the afternoon. The people here still do what the indigenous people did and what my people and all of the first European immigrants did: make a living from the land. It hasn't been turned into a Kmart or paved over for suburban development. No pumpjacks dot the landscape.

There are plenty of differences, of course. Early settlers farmed only one or two acres at first, working their way up to several. It was damn hard to plow up virgin prairie sod with its deep roots. And they often planted wheat, a crop that requires less moisture. The farmers are in the fields today, probably planting corn. Prices are so high, why wouldn't they? Some of that corn will no doubt be used to produce ethanol.

We don't have petrochemicals in Minnesota, so we grow corn for ethanol. Homegrown alternative energy! I should be enthused about ethanol, but the production plants are water and energy hogs.

I call T. J., and he says he's dropping off his last load and will be back at the farm by about 5:30. He invites me to go to the farmstead and photograph the old log home and wait for him there.

His driveway is long, and a big transmission line passes right over it. Is it the same line that generated so much controversy? I park near the house. My car is six years old, but it's almost certainly the newest vehicle on the place. Several old cars and tractors constitute an *in situ* farm museum. T. J. has said he doesn't farm anymore, and if you're driving a semi all over the Midwest, you must not worry much about old tractors lying around. And maybe he's nostalgic.

I don't see the log house, but it has to be here. I walk toward the farm fields, away from the county road. A little black kitty appears out of nowhere and joins me.

Well away from the parking area—behind a pile of scrap lumber, backdrop to a dead car and tucked into a grove of scrub trees—is the homesteader shack where my grandfather was born in 1886. The dovetail corner joints are more than a little wobbly. Dovetail joints require skill to construct, but they don't require nails. Nail-free construction might have been a plus for the cash-poor Jonssons who became the cash-poor Westbergs after they reached Minnesota.

Ten years after my immigrant clan arrived in North America, Oscar's grandfather Johannes proved up a homestead here. He would have been fifty-one and Inge forty-five. Not that I know anything about homesteading, but that seems a little old. First off, you have to build a home and live in it to satisfy the U.S. government that you're serious about settling this land. I can't say with certainty that my people built this log house, but it seems likely. Of course, Johannes had his two sons, one of them Oscar's father, John Jr. The two boys would have been old enough to do some of the work.

And just seven years later, Oscar was born in this log house. His parents might have sought help from a midwife, a family member, or a neighbor for the birth, but they didn't have the luxury of electric lights or electric anything. What did they use to light up the birthing bed? Kerosene lamps? And what did they do for heat? Oscar was born in late March, month six of a typical Minnesota winter. This was less than a hundred and fifty years ago but already well beyond my comprehension and comfort level. We're so soft today, and we city folks are even softer.

T. J. has left the sliding door to the log house open for me so I can take photos. Entering this place requires courage because it's filled with leaning, stacked, or tipping-over stuff. T. J. told me on the phone the other day that the log house had been altered in the hundred and thirty-five years since my ancestors built it, pressed into service as a storage locker for livestock, tractors, chickens, wood, and grain. I can barely take in or interpret all the stuff stored in here, but I am especially struck by the eviscerated piano. I wasn't expecting a piano. It reminds me how hard it is to pretend you understand people from the past by studying bare-bones public records. Did my grandfather play the piano? This piano?

Viewing the past through a public records filter is one thing. But if I view the past through my cheap-fossil-fuel glasses, the adze marks on these logs stand out. Nobody fired up an electric saw to build this home. To achieve straight edges on the logs, someone had to use an adze. The gashes are everywhere. Maybe the neighbors helped. This place was small but solid.

Wooden pegs and adze marks on the white oak logs of Oscar's childhood home, built in the 1870s. Lisa Westberg Peters

Today, of course, it doesn't look too solid. The logs have shrunk so that there are gaps between them. They're gray and weathered, and in many places the logs have been replaced with more modern boards.

T. J. finally arrives, driving his semi, of course! He parks it adeptly off to the side of his driveway and walks toward me, beaming. He has lived here all his life and relishes meeting someone who is connected to its past. We walk back to the log house. He speculates about whether it had a sod roof and says that the original squared-off logs are white oak and came from Douglas County, about twenty miles northeast of here.

Later, at his dining room table, T. J. shows me a poster board about the log house, a school project created by his son. The fact that a schoolchild created a poster about my family's homestead helps push me away from my earlier position of mild flabbergastion to pleasure. My gang did it. They weighed the promises of the promoters and the hucksters, they came all this way, and they homesteaded, goddammit, on good Minnesota black dirt.

I ask T. J. about the power line.

Is it the same line that people protested in the '70s?

Oh yeah, he says, nodding vigorously.

Did you protest? I ask.

Nope, he says.

He was fine with the line crossing his land. And of course, the power utilities compensated him. He says, grinning, that he lived for quite a while on those payments.

A branch of the oxcart trail once crossed his land, too, he says. When he was a kid, he could see the depressions in the ground left by the wheels of the carts. Things start to click in my head: the Westbergs might have picked up this very trail in St. Paul.

T. J. says the tracks are gone now. The virgin prairie is under cultivation.

By the time I leave, I feel as though this seventy-eight-year-old retired farmer, a perfect stranger to me, is a friend. I invite him to call the next time he's driving through Minneapolis. Stop in for dinner. He's half-Swedish and half-Norwegian, mixed like me. *I have to take pills for the Swede half,* he jokes. And we both laugh because I've made similar jokes.

As I leave, the sky is more heavily overcast and the light low. You can't see western North Dakota from here, but I'm sure the parched winds of the Dust Bowl dumped North Dakota topsoil here. Farming practices have changed, but blizzards today might still carry North Dakota soil across state lines. Sometimes in Minneapolis we get saturated red sunsets when the winds carry a lot of dust from the plains or smoke from fires in Canada.

It's 7:30, I haven't eaten anything for several hours, and I've had to pee for the past three.

I don't get very far when I see a tiny country cemetery, and I slam on the brakes. I should have guessed. All those Swedish Lutheran immigrants needed a place to bury their dead.

My dad hated cemeteries. *Waste of space!* he always said. I, on the other hand, love cemeteries. They're quiet places to lie in the grass, feel the ghosts, and admire—free for nothing— slab after slab of gorgeous granite.

A flag whips in the wind, but the pioneer church is gone. The good people of Swan Lake Township, some of them no doubt related to me, have erected a plaque telling who is buried here and where to find their graves. Westbergs! My clan, buried right here for years, and I never knew it.

I unlatch the gate and walk into the cemetery. And there it is, a big Westberg headstone and two gravestones for Oscar's parents, John Jr. and Carrie. There should have been more graves. What about his grandparents, Johannes and Inge, the Swedish pioneers? I start poking into the thick sod with a Swiss Army knife.

After a minute or so of random stabs at the turf, the knife clinks against something hard an inch or so down. I cut away the sod and find another grave marker. There he is. Johannes. Looks like he died in 1909, forty years after immigrating, long enough to reach the American dream. He fed his family! The fish jumped for him!

I poke that Swiss Army knife into the ground all over the place, convinced I'll find Inge's grave, but there are no more stone markers near the Westberg headstone. She has to be buried somewhere, right? But it's clear I'm not going to find her today, and I still have to pee.

For the moment, the wind has died down. The dust kicked up by farmers driving their massive machines—their names and functions unknown to me—has settled. Even the flag isn't whipping around as much, but ten or so windmills spin madly on the western horizon.

DOUGLAS COUNTY, MINNESOTA

I park on a winding gravel road and walk uphill on a path to find Inge's burial site, which overlooks patches of woods, a farm field, and a lake named Oscar. Yes, Lake Oscar.

I learned the fate of Oscar's grandmother from a local historian. It wasn't especially satisfying.

Inge died, probably in childbirth, on another branch of the old oxcart trail, just twenty miles from the promised land in Stevens County. The members of a Lutheran congregation of Swedish settlers buried her here. No wonder I couldn't find her gravestone with my Swiss Army knife.

Not only did this brave immigrant die soon after catching

Abandoned pioneer cemetery in Douglas County, Minnesota, the burial site of my great-great-grandmother, Ingeborg Ersdotter, who died around 1872. Lisa Westberg Peters

Nord Amerika fever, but the pioneer cemetery she was buried in eventually was abandoned.

I hate that. So many things conspire to cut the ropes that connect me to my past. Illiteracy. Abandoned cemeteries.

Today this cemetery has been reduced to a few trees, a scattered collection of unreadable gravestones, and a monument erected by local residents who were also bothered by the severed connection to the past. The rest of the cemetery is a cornfield.

Inge left behind a baby girl. Many years later, as the story goes, this country girl left home, boarded a train bound for Minneapolis, and disappeared.

POOLING

It is agreed that this lease is in force on said leased premises or on acreage pooled therewith . . .

Pooling is the practice of combining mineral owners in a specified area to develop oil and gas resources in a more orderly, efficient, and less environmentally damaging way. Pooled mineral owners share in a well's proceeds. Pools are typically formed by mineral developers, but in some cases the state forces mineral owners to join a pool in a process similar to eminent domain.

WILLIAMS COUNTY, NORTH DAKOTA
Oscar's grandfather homesteaded in western Minnesota, but that wasn't nearly the end of the family's drive to make its mark on the plains.

I stop my car next to a slough alongside County Road 12. The countryside is not perfectly flat, and the Little Muddy River winds its little muddy way through the fields to the Missouri River. If I've counted miles correctly, this slough is on land where the next two generations of Westbergs—Oscar and his father, John Jr.—homesteaded in the early 1900s. A few ducks paddle around in it. A sandpiper scolds me from the power lines. I'm near her nest, or maybe she's just a crank.

Uncle Rich and I had this exchange a few days ago.

Did you know that both your dad and grandfather homesteaded near Alamo? Alamo is a tiny farming community about forty miles northeast of Williston.

No, he says.

You didn't? I ask, incredulous.

Walt and I never heard anything about it. Dad never talked about it.

Uncle Rich's mind is a storehouse as loaded with memories

as the Bakken Shale is with oil. But he can't remember things he never knew in the first place.

Descending from homesteaders should be a point of pride— it is for me!—but Oscar never mentioned it to his sons. I don't know why he chose deliberate silence, but I do know it's another way to sever the connections.

And why did he and his father leave western Minnesota, where they could have made a good living farming? And remember, oil wouldn't be discovered in western North Dakota for another half century.

Rich can't help me, so I've had to consult my enormous and growing stash of old documents. When I lay papers on the floor in a giant square, the patchwork resembles a farmer's crop map: quarter section of census forms; half section of land deeds; a quarter section here, a quarter section there of town histories, obituaries, and newspaper articles. I finally piece together the reasons from both facts and speculation.

I had to dig for the facts. The speculation I am entitled to. I've moved a few times, the most memorable occasion being a trip halfway across the continent with two cars, two children, a spouse, a cat, and no cell phones. It was a trip interrupted by an emergency stop for a pet tranquilizer in Glendive, Montana (*It's me or the cat is how I put it at the freeway exit*), and several stops for house sale negotiations conducted at pay phones. Moving is hell, or surreal, or something. You should always have more than one reason to move. The Westberg gang had at least three:

Crowded conditions

After the immigrants settled in western Minnesota, two of Oscar's aunts married, and each produced ten children. Their progeny alone were enough for a couple of country baseball teams, I don't know how many threshing crews, or in this clan's case, a family orchestra. But those 160-acre homesteads in western Minnesota weren't big enough for the lot of them.

My grandfather, back row center, a young violinist in the family
orchestra, Stevens County, Minnesota, around 1900. Family photo

In the early 1900s, free land out west seemed like a perfect
solution to crowded conditions.

Business, business, business
When Oscar's immigrant grandfather was seventy-two years
old, he told a U.S. census taker that he was a capitalist. A
capitalist! I'm not sure what you have to be doing to declare
yourself a capitalist at age seventy-two. But he sure showed
capitalist instincts when he eventually sold his four-buck
homestead property to Oscar's father for $1,000. A tidy profit!

So. Immigrant Capitalist Father hands down his 160-acre
farm to Son, but he doesn't give it away; he sells it. New rules
in Nord Amerika!

Johannes declared himself a capitalist, but it was Oscar's
father, John Jr., who actually opened a business. John Jr.
homesteaded in western North Dakota and also started up a

hardware store in Alamo. He advertised it in the fledgling local newspaper as *a new and complete line of hardware, Furniture and Auto Supplies, Harness, oils and paints. Call and see Us.* Imagine how excited he must have been, how many hours he spent planning the enterprise.

The editor of the paper certainly thought well of the town's entrepreneurs. *No bigger hearted, or more enthusiastic, body of hustling business men can be found than the ones whose lot it is to build up and give publicity to the infant city of the west.* The infant city of the west even had a Ford dealership by 1910, just two years after Henry Ford invented the Model T and three years before he invented the assembly line.

I don't have any small-business bones in my body. If there's a gene for that, I didn't inherit it. But starting a small business is a very American thing to do. Many years ago on a trip to Europe, I enthusiastically invited a Danish gentleman to visit our country, but he told me he wasn't especially interested. The United States was all *business, business, business.* His sour pronouncement left me thinking, *Well! Maybe you Danes could learn a little from us!*

Adventure

At the turn of the twentieth century, newspaper readers in Stevens County read ads like this: *I have some Choice Lands for sale in North Dakota . . . You know I am reliable to deal with. See me at once.* The promoter's urgent assurances of reliability send my thoughts in the opposite direction, but that's just my journalistic skepticism.

The prospect of Choice Lands in North Dakota pulled hard on thousands of Scandinavian settlers in western Minnesota, and it must have pulled hard on Oscar, his father, and several of their neighbors and relatives. Oscar had given high school a try for a year, even tried teaching in a one-room schoolhouse, but book learning and teaching didn't light his fire.

In the early 1900s, a gang of farmers from Stevens County—

Oscar and his father may have been the youngest and oldest at eighteen and forty-one—filed on claims in northwestern North Dakota, and their claims were so close to each other that a highlighter smudge for each on my township map turns the cluster of claims into an orange prairie flower.

As Oscar began his new life, he was probably already in love with a young woman who lived near his family's Minnesota farm, and that must have been part of his plan: get established as a North Dakota farmer and then bring his bride out there. But she was no delicate prairie flower and did not wait to be summoned. She homesteaded, too, right across the township line from her beau.

Think of it. You're young and your whole life is ahead of you. Dave and I fell under the same spell when we were new parents. We yanked ourselves away from our native state of Minnesota to live for several years on the West Coast.

Why are you leaving? our friends asked with quizzical expressions.

Adventure! we declared. And that was it, pure and simple. We packed up our baby and our cat, our hiking boots and our tent, and bought raincoats when we got there.

I get it. I get the desire to bust loose and try something new. Like a rope in a blinding snowstorm, it connects me to this place I struggle to feel connected to and to these otherwise distant people.

By the way, this bride of Oscar's was not my grandmother.

The new Stevens County—and all—homesteaders must have pooled their resources to buy farm machinery and combined their talents to help each other with any number of farming tasks: building homestead shacks, harvesting the crops, tending to the cooking when someone's kids were sick or when babies were born.

In a two-volume tome called *The Wonder of Williams,* there

are stories of homesteaders finding rings of stones when they plowed up the prairie sod. Indigenous people had to adapt to the harsh living conditions here; the stones anchored tipis against the wind.

The Stevens County settlers also banded together for treacherous trips through the snow to nearby coal mines. You can't burn wood for fuel in western North Dakota (very few trees), buffalo dung was probably becoming scarce, and oil wasn't on anyone's radar at the time, but lignite was everywhere.

Five years after staking their claims, the Stevens County

Picnickers in Alamo, North Dakota, around 1918; Oscar in straw hat, second from right. Family photo

homesteaders made the trip to Williston by wagon to prove up. *The Wonder of Williams* relates the story, told, no doubt, by descendants of one of the gang:

> They took lunch along and camped along the trail while the horses had a rest and feed. The sun was blazing hot and there was no shade to be found. Those thirty-five miles seemed endless but at last town was reached and the travelers got rooms at the Great Northern Hotel. The heat was so intense that it was impossible to rest.
>
> When they had left home on Sunday the crop was nice and green and in the heading stage. There had been no moisture since the winter snows, which had brought the crop along so far. On Monday, some of the men filed while others did so on Tuesday, after which they set out for home again. The heat was still unbearable and when they reached home they found the crops all burned up by the heat except for the low places. There wasn't much to be done but "grin and bear it," a thing which they had to do many times in the long years that followed.

From my parked car on the shoulder of County Road 12, I see farm field after farm field, but no oil wells. There are quite a few south, west, and east of here. I don't know why I'm not seeing wells, but I'm starting to believe that the decision to drill is based in part on geology and in part on tradition, hunch, rumor, and chance.

I can't see any homesteaders' shacks, either. They must have fallen down long ago or were plowed under to accommodate farm machinery. Occasionally I do see shacks as I drive across the state. Their weathered boards allow in plenty of North Dakota sunshine, and they lean as if pushed by the wind.

In January 2008, *National Geographic* magazine ran haunting photos of these and other dilapidated structures across this remote countryside. You've heard of ghost towns. The *National Geographic* photos made North Dakota look like a ghost state. I sent the article to my parents; they hated it.

In a letter to the editor of the magazine, Governor John Hoeven jabbed an angry finger. What about our thriving ethanol and biodiesel facilities? He jabbed again. And the "moan of the wind" you talked about? *That same wind is on its way to producing nearly 1000 megawatts of clean renewable energy on commercial wind farms across North Dakota.* We have pasta manufacturing, pheasant hunting, on and on . . . *There is a mood of optimism across the land.*

His rant didn't surprise me. A governor should be a state's Chief Booster and Defender. What I find most interesting now is that he went to great lengths to brag about renewable energy and barely mentioned oil. Just a few months after the article ran, the U.S. Geological Survey issued a vastly higher estimate of oil reserves in the Bakken, and interest in North Dakota's oil skyrocketed.

Governor Hoeven wasn't making up that bit about optimism early in 2008, but today's *mood of optimism* at the North Dakota state capitol has nothing to do with renewable energy.

If you don't count the cranky bird, it's silent here. I can see why the noise and volume of the oil-field truck traffic has been such an adjustment for North Dakotans long accustomed to this deep silence. There is the noise of the tractors, of course, the massive machinery that shoots seeds from a tank into tubes where they're dropped onto the ground in long perfect rows. But the incessant oil-field traffic, it's different somehow.

It's so peaceful today, you could almost forget the blizzards, the prairie fires, and the pioneers' scorched crops. A water truck just went past on Highway 50, but I doubt it's on its way to put out a fire. I'm sure an oil well is being fracked somewhere.

As my ancestors and thousands of other Scandinavian immigrants settled in western North Dakota in the early 1900s and started to work their claims, a far different movement was under way at the southern end of the Great Plains: the nation's first oil boom, Texas born and bred. In North Dakota, nobody was looking for oil yet, but wildcatters—the cowboy types who drill without any documented proof that the good stuff is nearby—were finding tantalizing evidence of natural gas.

Oscar's first job in North Dakota, besides farming and a brief stint at an Alamo bank, was county treasurer. He must have inherited his sense of civic involvement from his father, who ran for constable and served as a township supervisor and fire warden in Stevens County.

There's a large photo of my grandfather, Oscar Westberg, on the front page of the first issue of the *Alamo Farmer* published on November 3, 1916. And he's handsome! *Republican nominee for Treasurer of Williams County*, says the ad. *Your influence and vote will be appreciated. General Election, Nov. 7, 1916.* Oscar would have been thirty, married, and working his homestead.

North Dakota's early experiment with Socialist-leaning policies via the Nonpartisan League had just begun. The league's organizers tried to maintain their ties with the Republican Party, but I don't think Oscar fell for any of that. He was a standard-issue Republican, whatever that meant in 1916.

And he would certainly have been reading all the local newspapers. In 1916, he would have read about his victory in the election and the first serious effort to drill for oil in North Dakota.

The Pioneer Oil and Gas Company obtained permits to drill three miles east of Williston and invited the people of Williston to come on out to take a look at their camp and drilling derricks. Oscar, who moved his young family from Alamo to Williston, might have taken them up on the offer. The *Willis-*

ton Herald quoted the company's manager in August of 1916 as saying, *If we are able to secure gas and oil as has been predicted by several experienced oil men then Williston will have a new industry which will prove vastly helpful in the future development of the community.*

The *Williston Graphic* reported about a month later that the company would try to prove that the *Williston district is destined to be among the largest natural gas producing areas of the United States, to say nothing of the possibilities for this city in the event that oil is struck.*

To say nothing!

The company drilled down about two thousand feet, struck water, and that was the end of that.

1916. The year the first oil well was drilled in North Dakota. That was the cart. The horse, literally and figuratively, came along the next year.

A U.S. Geological Survey scientist, A. J. Collier, set out to explore the North Dakota countryside on horseback the following summer. He was mapping coal beds, which are everywhere in western North Dakota. Along the way, he discovered a geological structure that made oil drillers, speculators, wildcatters, and no doubt a few con men salivate. In 1917, Collier discovered an anticline. Think of an anticline as an upside-down canoe, that is, a domed lid of impermeable rock. When oil is deep in the earth, it tends to rise, but if it encounters one of these impermeable lids, it stops rising.

Wouldn't it be great, I thought, to read Collier's notes, his first thoughts about the geologic structure that changed the course of North Dakota's—and let's not forget my own family's—history? Collier might also describe what it was like to travel through the Missouri River bluff country by horseback.

But his field notes have disappeared. A half-dozen people who work for such institutions as the North Dakota Geological Survey, the University of North Dakota, and Collier's own employer, the U.S. Geological Survey—people who should know—do not know where the notes are. I'm hoping that this very public lament—*Hey! Where are Collier's field notes?*—will prompt someone to take the time to dig around and find them in a basement filing cabinet.

I did, however, get my hands on the next best thing: the field notes of another geologist, A. G. Leonard, the first director of the North Dakota Geological Survey, who studied similar territory at the same time. Once in a while, the two geologists and their survey parties ran into each other and camped together.

Leonard bought two horses, Rock and Rowdy, for $325 at the start of his trip. He doesn't say how much he paid for the rest of his supplies, but I'm guessing he paid top dollar for the big cast-iron frying pan, which now anchors a shelf at the University of North Dakota's geology library.

> Aug 9 Went down to Missouri River . . . where Collier's party was camped. The Fort Union (coal) beds are finely exposed in the bluffs and ravines . . .
>
> Aug 10 Met Collier's party this morning, and together we went down Plum Creek valley to the river bottom.

Over the course of several days, they occasionally shared a campfire and stories in the evenings. A photo of their combined survey teams shows six men sitting or standing in a canvas tent held up by a log pressed into service as a tent pole. The poor quality of the photo obscures most of the men's faces, but there they are, scientists in the field. Dr. Leonard sits in the middle in a white shirt, his hands folded, and Collier, on the far right, wears a dark suit and tie and sports a pointy beard and a gentlemanly look. Once again, I'm struck by the formal clothes that people wore. When I camp, I wear hooded sweatshirts and jeans.

Collier's notes have gone missing, but he did write a letter to Dr. Leonard the following year, referring to the summer of 1917:

> We camped on the riverbank during one of those heavy windstorms early in September and had an opportunity to see how much dust can be blown into the air at such times. A great many of the deposits near the Missouri might be accounted for as wind-blown material. We were all sorry to miss you south of the river.

Dave and I once camped on this same stretch of the Missouri River at Lewis and Clark State Park. Our tent nearly blew away during the night. We had to weigh down one corner with a cooler, another with a pack. And Collier was right: a great many of the deposits in our tent were definitely windblown material.

Nearly one hundred years after Collier and Leonard explored the Missouri River bluff country by horseback, I explore the same territory on Highway 1804, a road dubbed the Lewis and Clark Historic Trail. Today the countryside surrounding Highway 1804 no longer rumbles with the *immence herds of buffaloe* observed by the nineteenth-century explorers. It throbs with trucks. When I pull off the road to check my maps, a water tanker zips past at well over the speed limit and sends a load of sand and grit flying through my open window to settle on my dashboard. More windborne sediments.

And when I turn off the main road onto the gravel roads to check out a piece of land or an oil well, I pull off to the side right away and wait. If a hill or a turn just ahead blocks my visibility, waiting several minutes is the only way I know to assess the level of traffic on the road and calculate my odds of running headlong into a truck.

I see a turnoff and a sign advertising Juneberry pie. Good enough for me. Even better, this is one of the spots where Collier saw evidence of the anticline. The Tobacco Garden Creek wiggles through a low, marshy area just north of here and empties into the Missouri. There's water in the creek today. Behind it, a layer cake of sedimentary rocks forms a steep bluff. I can't see the tilt in the sediments that Collier saw, but I have neither the skills nor the best vantage point.

Collier's notes may be missing, but he later published a paper on his discovery:

> The rocks of North Dakota in general lie nearly flat; anticlines or domes are not easily detected.

But Collier did detect this anticline and named it for the tiny post office of Nesson, which no longer exists. What he guessed wrong was the anticline's potential for oil:

> . . . it is the writer's opinion that the chances of finding oil in the Nesson anticline are very small.

Exposed layers of sedimentary rock in the bluffs near the site where the Nesson Anticline was identified in 1917. Lisa Westberg Peters

He was aiming too shallow, says Ed Murphy, North Dakota's chief geologist, given the formations that he mentioned. But it hardly mattered that Collier had dumped on the prospects of finding oil. The wildcatters and speculators read the word "anticline," and they were off to the races.

It's not likely my grandfather saw this scientific paper, and the word "anticline" didn't appear in the lay press until later. Besides, in 1917, he was busy being county treasurer. He had moved to Williston with his young wife, Anna, and their two children, and they were about to have a third. Oscar was starting to focus on his new job, paying the county's bills for such things as drayage (that is, transport via horse-drawn cart), postage, and chimney cleaning at the jail.

My grandfather moved away from the Stevens County homesteading gang to conduct county business, but I doubt his fever of optimism had broken. He probably rented out his homestead land and eased into the role of gentleman farmer.

I'm grateful for this rest stop, this old ferry landing where pie is now a big attraction. There aren't many places to pull off 1804 and definitely not many places to buy a piece of pie packed with Juneberries, which taste like a delicious cross between blueberries and cherries.

Lots of oil around here, I say to the proprietor.

She smiles. *We love it.*

I laugh. *I'll bet you do.*

We don't have any land, she adds. But she does have Juneberry pie all year long, and she says the truckers can drive past her pie sign only so many times before they have to stop in to try it.

I want to buy a whole pie because I'm so hungry, but when she asks if I have an oven, I scale down and buy one piece already baked. Just for fun, I ask her if she has ever heard of the Nesson Anticline. She shakes her head but explains that she is a recent transplant. And I doubt the oil-field truck drivers, whose jobs can be traced to the discovery of this structure that runs north and south through western North Dakota for seventy-five miles, take their eyes off the road in order to enjoy the layer-cake bluffs; at least I hope they don't.

My grandfather didn't know about anticlines when he started up as county treasurer, but in the early 1940s, everyone knew about the oil-trapping structure. By then, Oscar was no longer young, but he bought farmland a few miles from here, just north, just over there, just beyond those bluffs.

Earlier I asked a North Dakota geologist to construct a map for me showing both the anticline and my grandfather's land parcels, and sure enough, Oscar's land was right smack on the axis of the anticline.

Why did Oscar buy farmland so late in his life? I ask Uncle Rich.

He wanted to be his own boss, Rich says. *He had been working for years for two old nurses at the hospital . . .*

My uncle leaves the sentence unfinished, but he doesn't need to finish it. *Two old nurses . . .* enough said.

He wasn't trying to cash in on the oil excitement? I ask.

Dad wanted to get out of working for everybody else. He wanted to be his own boss, Rich repeats, ever patient with me and my pesky questions.

FORCE MAJEURE CLAUSE

> Whenever as a result of war, rebellion, riots, strikes, lockouts, acts of God, or adverse weather conditions the oil company, despite its good faith effort, is prevented from exercising any rights or performing any obligations under this lease, this lease shall remain in full force and effect . . .

> *Each lease will spell out which events allow a mineral developer to halt production while still keeping a lease active.*

WILLIAMS COUNTY, NORTH DAKOTA

It's 7:24 in the morning and already hazy. I head north on Highway 85 out of Williston. I see the usual mix of farms and oil wells. The highway crosses the Little Muddy River several times. They should rename it the Little Twisty-Turny River.

After twenty-five miles or so, I turn right on Highway 50, drive past a huge alkaline lake, and turn left into the tiny town of Alamo. I have directions from here, but I still miss the next turn. I wind up on a gravel road, hugging the north side of another big lake, and then the road disappears underwater, so I turn back and stop at the nearest farmhouse to ask directions. An elderly woman directs me to the gravel road just a quarter mile back.

I take it, but I wonder whether my car is too low slung for the bristly bushes in the middle of the road. I don't think it's a mile before I see it, a tender country cemetery in countryside so remote, it could be the steppes of central Asia.

The sweet music that lured my grandfather west from Minnesota stopped here. Oscar's entire first family is buried in this cemetery: his young wife, Anna Caroline, and his three young children.

No doubt about it, this pioneering stuff was especially

hard on women and children. Per's wife, Beret, in *Giants in the Earth,* lost her mind somewhere between the blizzards and the endless horizon. And of course, my own ancestor Inge died in childbirth and left behind a baby girl twenty miles from their homestead site.

I am now an old pro at cleaning off gravestones, but it takes me a while to clear away the grass and roots. I stay much longer than I anticipated because it's so pleasant. Nobody, absolutely nobody, is about. A flock of blackbirds scolds me as if I were intruding on their incredibly private space, and I'm reminded of the sandpiper that chewed me out earlier.

In the space of three years—1913 to 1916—Oscar and his bride, his childhood sweetheart from western Minnesota, had three children, including the first baby girl to be born in the pioneer town of Alamo. Imagine the celebrating among the Stevens County gang. Maybe friends and relatives came round in twos and threes to visit, dropping off a handmade baby gift.

In less than half that time, just sixteen months, Oscar's toddler son, infant daughter, and wife succumbed to pneumonia, an unspecified *long and severe illness,* and tuberculosis. The oldest son, Vincent, had TB, too, but he survived until he was a teenager. I can't grasp such personal tragedy; it's far out of the range of what I consider to be a normal midwestern life. An obituary, no doubt written by Anna's overwrought family members, offers a glimpse of the sadness that began with little Harald's sickness:

> The young mother's tender devotion and anxiety would not allow her to rest and she lavished upon [Harald] all loving care and attention. Those trying weeks, however, were too much for her and her health broke down. Gradually in her weakened condition, tuberculosis, that dreaded white plague, set in.

"White plague," a term I'd never heard, referred to how pale tuberculosis patients became. At the time Anna died, TB was one of the leading causes of death in the United States. Doctors and scientists didn't understand the pathology of the disease, and because they didn't, treatment was misguided.

In lieu of effective treatment, Oscar, who must have been desperate, sent Anna to the state's tuberculosis sanatorium in Dunseith, North Dakota, more than halfway across the state. He later sent his frail wife to stay with his brother's family in

Country cemetery near Alamo, North Dakota, where Oscar's entire first family is buried. Lisa Westberg Peters

the dry Arizona climate, and that's where she was when her babies died. Anna's sister and a hired nurse cared for the children, but it wasn't enough.

If I had written the obituary for Anna, I might have loaded it up with active verbs:

> Neighbors streamed into the church . . . County government officials abandoned their work for the day . . . Oscar Westberg buried his young wife and the mother of his children under the spring sunshine.

But the family chose the soporific voice so typical of obituaries, a voice that eases into its subject—in this case, death—and they managed to convey the esteem the community held for the new county treasurer and his young wife:

> The church was filled to overflowing with the grief-stricken neighbors from Alamo and Williston, coming to pay their last respects to the dead. The courthouse was closed Wednesday afternoon and the county officials were present at the funeral. Interment was made in the Alamo cemetery.

Six years earlier in his hometown of Kensington, Minnesota, Oscar had almost certainly promised Anna he would take care of her. Young lovers used to do that, and today they still take on this sense of obligation.

Our future son-in-law reassured us just hours after emigrating from Spain that he would take care of our daughter. He was groggy and hungry, but he wanted to repeat in our presence the promise he must have already made to our daughter. We marveled later at this declaration, not for its content but for his presence of mind after such a long flight.

This twenty-first-century young man's obligation to deliver on his promise needs no exception for tuberculosis or any number of other infectious diseases. He and all of us now understand the value of antibiotics, clean drinking water, and effective sewage treatment systems. This doesn't mean it will be easy for him to deliver on his promise. It never is.

Dad and Rich didn't know where Vincent was being taken when he went away. Nobody ever mentioned the sanatorium, and Oscar never talked about the rest of his first family.

We often drove out to the cemetery on Memorial Day, Uncle Rich says.

To visit the graves, I say.

Dad did. We stayed in the car and waited for him.

My mouth drops. *You sat in the car while Oscar stood at the graves?* I'm tempted to ask. But how would I feel if I were wife number two, accompanying my spouse on a visit to the graves of wife number one and his first family? Rich says that Meg, his mother and my grandmother, probably discouraged talk of the first family. I don't know what it was like for her. Best to back off. But waiting for your grieving husband and making your little boys wait in a hot car when there were grasshoppers to chase in the cemetery, that's puzzling.

I retrace my route along the bristle-brush road and drive back to the town of Alamo, but I hesitate to stop. Alamo is so small, residents notice a stranger's car. This town is where Oscar's dad, John Jr., set up his hardware store and where many others established businesses on faith more than a hundred years ago. The businesses are gone now. I take a picture of the grain elevator and a dilapidated building that could easily have housed John Jr.'s ill-fated hardware store.

I see two women in front of the post office and stop to ask a few questions. They're friendly—of course. These are native North Dakotans. One of them offers to take me over to the Lutheran church on Main Street to search for my family in the old records. I don't know what she had in mind for this morning, but she willingly wastes a good half hour on me.

She says that she and her husband grow wheat around here.

There isn't any oil drilling yet in their area, she adds, but it will come. She seems to have the North Dakotan shrug mentality about it. She did say they were getting more and more oil patch traffic through town. I don't see any trucks now—there's no traffic at all—as we cross the street to the church.

The headings on the record book's pages proclaim in Norwegian the date of death—*dodsdatum*—and the burial date—*jordfaestede*. We pore over the ledger in the tiny church office, flip the pages slowly, and finally we find them, Oscar's infant children, their names and their deaths recorded in elegant handwritten script. There's nothing elegant, though, about burying a small child in a remote country cemetery on the northern plains. Nothing. And no parent ever wants to outlive a child.

When my girls were very young, they got away from me somehow—I don't know how—on separate occasions, and I had to leap up, run, and yank them out of bodies of water. One had started dog-paddling in the frigid waters of Puget Sound just a few feet from shore and was blissfully unaware she was in real danger. To reach her, I covered ten feet of beach so quickly, she couldn't have dog-paddled for more than a few seconds. It was still too long. The other I pulled out of a swimming pool before she had even begun to flail or dog-paddle.

I probably can't make a strong case that I came close to outliving my daughters. But those are the moments that for years afterward send you into a complete body sweat whenever you think of them.

The Scandinavians who founded this church paid careful attention to these tragedies, and they knew that the rituals accompanying them tended to soothe. Today this elegant handwritten script soothes me.

As I wait to turn right on Highway 50 to return to Williston, an oil-field truck zooms past. This one carries sand for hydraulic fracturing.

The go-west music begins again, slowly perhaps, but still hopeful.

In 1919, less than a year after his first wife died, Oscar took out a $2,500 loan on his homestead property, the equivalent of almost $34,000 today. He still owned the land, but he must have been renting out the fields. The farmer renting the land would have needed machinery, granaries, seed.

Hold that thought. Hefty mortgage on the farm.

Around the same time, he started a Ford dealership in Williston. When I pay attention to how much both my dad and Uncle Rich talked about the cars of their childhood and teen years, I don't need the state's historians to tell me that the invention of the automobile, particularly Henry Ford's affordable Model T, was a big hairy deal to North Dakotans. New Yorkers? What did they need of cars? They were all jammed together in tight spaces. But North Dakotans had miles to go before they could reach neighbors, buy a tractor, and attend to sick family. The automobile chipped away at that isolation.

Oscar must have fallen in love with the affordable Model T the same as everyone else. He was living in town, county treasuring, and courting a woman who could possibly serve as a mother for his son. Why not start a car dealership? Well, one reason I can think of with my hindsight glasses is that agriculture prices were just about to crash at the end of World War I, giving North Dakota a decade-long head start on the Great Depression. Such timing.

And that wasn't all. The Ford Motor Company had told Oscar that he needed to pay for the twenty cars he had taken on consignment whether he sold them to customers or not. Oscar went bankrupt. I'm no authority on bankruptcy, and neither the folks in the federal bankruptcy court nor the National Archives could cough up any records from that long ago, so I don't know why he was able to hang onto his homestead land. But he did.

Oscar married my grandmother Meg a year and a half after

My grandparents Oscar Westberg and Magna (Meg)
Monson were married by her father in Hazen,
North Dakota, in 1919. Family photo

his first wife died. Meg was a preacher's kid in Williston. Some
preacher's kids rebel in an extreme way against their parents'
strict rules. They go up when they're told to go down. My
grandmother, at least while she was raising children, embraced
the strictness: no liquor, no dancing, no card games because
they might resemble gambling, and no going out with girls. *We
got clobbered with Bibles, testaments, and Sunday school,* wrote
my father.

But Meg was also a gifted musician—a singer, pianist, and
organist—and came from a musical family. Oscar loved music,
too. He'd played the violin in the Stevens County family or-

chestra, and he loved to sing. But I wonder if this was a marriage of convenience. Oscar needed a mother for his son; Meg was facing spinsterhood at the ripe old age of twenty-seven. Maybe practicality was the spark, music the fire.

Dad and Rich were born in rapid succession soon afterward. Their father needed a job, any kind of job, to support his growing family, and he found work selling insurance, but the family had to leave Williston, hop-skipping across North Dakota: Minot, Devils Lake, Fargo. And he must have had

Uncle Rich, left, and my father, eleven months apart and raised like twins, Williston, North Dakota, around 1923. Family photo

some initial success, my dad writes, because he bought a fancy 1921 Studebaker touring car (note: not a Ford). To be sure, he needed a reliable car for traveling the countryside and a nice-looking car to impress customers. Success at sales? It's possible. It's also possible that Oscar so loved cars, he made an intemperate purchase. He was diligently paying off his auto dealership creditors, paying on a farm mortgage, and now paying on a car loan.

While the family wandered across North Dakota, my grandfather heard another harsh *tap-tap-tap* of the baton that stops the music.

For failure to pay on his mortgage, Oscar lost his Alamo homestead property. He had acquired both his father's and his first wife's homesteads but he lost these as well, and the county sheriff eventually sold all of the properties. From optimistic start to dismal finish, the homesteading adventure lasted about a dozen years. I stray into territory out of my league when I make parallels to the recession that began in 2008, now dubbed the Great Recession, in which so many people lost homes, but who can resist straying once in a while? You introduce naïve, overly optimistic buyers to greedy or overly enthusiastic financiers, and if you do it on a grand scale, you get trouble.

Then the Marshall-Wells Hardware Company of Duluth, Minnesota, sued John Jr. for not paying for the inventory in his Alamo hardware store. *The defendant has absconded (with the goods) or has concealed himself; he has sold, assigned, transferred, secreted or otherwise disposed of the goods.* He has skedaddled to Seattle, the wronged party claimed, and pretty much can't be reached.

In one of the papers, the county sheriff certified that he had searched for the defendant and failed to find him. He even recorded how much he spent on gas ($29, which is about $404 today) in his search.

But the document that brings my paragraph skimming to a

sudden halt is the handwritten inventory of what remained in the hardware store in the fledgling town of Alamo. The sheriff must have gone through the store with a deputy and a clipboard. One of them identified the items; the other wrote them down. Seven graniteware pie pans at $1.15 each. Twenty-one pot covers at thirty-five cents each. As the list went on and on, the recorder grew weary of recording prices, or perhaps the items bore no price tag. Two posthole augurs. One rolling pin—old. One rosette iron (no doubt for the Scandinavian bakers at Christmas). Assortment—machine drive chains. Barn door latches "Alligator." Three trapdoor rings. One and a half pounds of six-inch wagon bolts. And upstairs, one hard coal base burner "Firefly" No. 716. The coal stove, which would have burned North Dakota lignite had anyone bought it, was listed alongside three child's rocking chairs.

The list is ten pages long.

John Jr. may have absconded with some of Marshall Wells's stuff, but he left a hell of a lot there.

I don't know what John Jr.'s side of this whole story was. The Westberg family's oral tradition signal on this event and all other events was very weak. Oscar never told his sons about his father's painful business failing.

Automobile fatalities in Minneapolis this year today had mounted to 20 with the death of John J. Westberg, 63 years old, 3131 Stevens avenue, who was run down at Washington avenue and Twelfth avenue S . . . According to a report of the accident, he was struck as he walked from the curb to board a streetcar. His skull was fractured and his body badly bruised.

MINNEAPOLIS JOURNAL, MAY 14, 1926

John Jr., my great-grandfather who emigrated from Sweden at age seven, was hit by a car at an intersection across the river from where I live. It's a half-hour stroll from my house.

John Jr.'s death certificate says he had been a common

laborer. All finished with farming, all finished with small business owning. It says he had lived in Minneapolis for the past three years, it doesn't say anything about absconding to Seattle, and one of the newspaper articles says he had been living with his two daughters. He had sold the Stevens County homestead land three years earlier.

And I can't know for sure what kind of car the reckless driver drove—the two newspaper articles didn't say—but it was probably a Model T. Henry Ford's Model T filled the streets at the time and eventually, of course, also contributed to the death of the streetcars.

Oscar provided the information for the coroner, and Oscar was known by all as a man with a sunny disposition. My dad remembered him as stern looking but jovial. He liked to tell jokes, had a sly sense of humor, and was optimistic, it goes without saying. He was like Uncle Rich, or I suppose it would be the reverse.

But as a young boy, my father saw Oscar crying in his den one night. My father assumed it was because of the family's precarious finances, and that must have been a large part of it.

By the late '20s, people weren't buying insurance. They were turning off their phones, then borrowing on their insurance policies or taking them out in cash, Uncle Rich says.

But I think Oscar was crying over much more than that. He had to have been crying over the relentless litany of failure and an impending tragedy: his son Vincent from his first marriage was near death.

North Dakota in the 1920s? It sucked. People left the state in droves.

Why didn't Oscar leave the state? I ask Uncle Rich.

He had Vincent at the sanatorium. Vincent kept him in North Dakota, he answers.

Of course, I say.

Oscar could hear music, but it was all funeral dirges.

MOTHER HUBBARD CLAUSE

This lease also covers and includes, in addition to that above described, all land, if any, contiguous or adjacent to or adjoining the land above described and (a) owned or claimed by the mineral owner by limitation, prescription, possession, reversion or unrecorded instrument, or (b) as to which the mineral owner has a preferential right of acquisition.

The oil company asks for the right to use adjacent property, property not specifically named in the lease. It protects the oil company against slight errors in the property description. The name of the clause refers to a mineral owner who goes to great lengths to satisfy the oil company, just as Mother Hubbard went to great lengths to satisfy her dog. The clause originated in Texas and typically isn't necessary in North Dakota oil leases today.

WILLIAMS COUNTY, NORTH DAKOTA

Several *forces majeures*—infectious disease, drought, economic meltdown—kicked my grandfather and his two young families over and over. After picturing this good and honest man crying in his den, I wanted my grandfather to kick some butt and not get kicked back.

I call my mother and ask my question again.

Why did Oscar buy farmland so late in life? Was it for the oil? Did he know about the potential for oil?

Just farming! she says, affirming Uncle Rich's assessment. *He was delighted to own land and farm it.*

I shouldn't try to rewrite history, and I need to remember that for most of the past sixty years, North Dakota oil was a pipsqueak prospect, not the bulky free agent it is today.

Throughout the 1920s and the 1930s, both the North Dakota oil wildcatters and my father outgrew their short pants and graduated to long pants.

1926

A North Dakotan named Jacobson got his hands on a pamphlet published by the state geologist identifying the Nesson Anticline as a good place to look for oil. Jacobson formed the Big Viking Oil Company—clever choice of a name with all those Norwegians in the state—to drill for oil beneath that anticline.

At the time, my father was just five. He was probably wearing shirts with Peter Pan collars, knickers, long stockings, and high-top shoes. He wasn't aware of anticlines, that's for sure.

1928

A newspaper article ran with this headline: "Oil Driller Is Sure Nesson Dome O.K." Nobody called the Nesson Anticline an upside-down canoe. The word "dome" was accurate enough and far easier for the headline writers to fit into one column. The reporter interviewed one of the Big Viking's employees who claimed that the Nesson dome had excellent prospects of being a source of oil and gas.

A newspaper ad reminded North Dakotans that they had, in fact, asked for drilling action, throwing responsibility for the risky operation onto their shoulders. *And here it is!* the company declared. *We've got drilling action!* You can almost see them pointing at the maps in front of them. The company quoted U.S. Geological Survey scientists saying that the area in the Nesson Anticline was the most favorable one to test first. And by the way, the company said, *make all checks payable to the Big Viking Oil Co.*

A year later, the company ran ads to beef up investor interest. *Big Viking Oil Meeting! A. M. McDaniel, the driller, will*

tell about the progress so far made and future prospects. We want
you there.

At the time, my father was in elementary school. His family moved from house to house, fifteen by my grandmother's
accounting.

No, it wasn't that many, says Uncle Rich.

But it was a lot, I say. *Why did you keep moving?*

Probably in search of cheaper rent, he says.

Of my father's homes that remain, all are modest, some
well maintained, some gone. One house burned down just a
few years ago.

One had a porch.

The screen is missing from the porch, Rich says.

You and Dad slept out there, didn't you? I say.

We put canvas on one end to keep the wind out.

Did you sleep there when it was cold? I ask.

He says yes.

That was a tuberculosis thing. People back then thought
you could avoid TB if you slept in the cold, fresh air. So these
two shy and obedient brothers sleep outside in the North Dakota elements at their parents' behest. That's the last time I
feel guilty about my daughters sleeping in the chilly lower level
of our split-entry house in St. Paul.

Rich doesn't say who pushed the porch-sleeping idea, his
mother or father, but my money is on Oscar. He lost his first
wife to TB; maybe he grabbed onto whatever folk wisdom
there was to keep his new family healthy, be it garlic to ward
off influenza or cold air to keep TB away.

My dad wrote in his memoirs that Oscar would heat up
bricks, wrap them in bath towels, and put the bricks in the
boys' bed to keep them warm. I'd like to inject here that the
long drought of written accounts that defines the first three
generations of American Westbergs breaks with my father.
After all the supposition, extrapolation, detective work, and

outright guessing I've had to do about my ancestors, Dad's memories printed out on his old dot-matrix printer feel like a warm brick at my feet. But those hard times—*Oh gosh, those years were real rough,* agrees Uncle Rich—left scars on my father's psyche and TB scars on his lungs.

1930

The year after the stock market crashed and the rest of the nation was feeling the misery North Dakota already knew, the Big Viking made a push to raise more money from the state's residents to bring the well to production. In other words, two years into the drilling, no oil.

The company held a bash at the well site. One photo shows people milling about a wooden oil derrick with Fords parked

Early wildcatters held open houses to celebrate and raise money for their risky drilling operations. Here, a large crowd listens to the music at the Big Viking Oil Company drilling rig near the Missouri River bluffs east of Williston, around 1930. Photographer unknown/State Historical Society of North Dakota

nearby and the badland bluffs of the Missouri River in the background. Another shows a band complete with tuba, horn, and clarinet players assembled for the festivities.

During these miserable years, hundreds of North Dakota farmers lost their land every year. It takes a certain amount of chutzpah to ask people bruised by the blows of the Depression to pitch in for such a speculative venture. But excitement about oil, however speculative, must have felt like a slim ray of hope to North Dakotans. *It is understood that the company holds about 20,000 acres of oil leases surrounding the well,* said the *Williston Herald.* Sick and tired of bad news, farmers signed over their mineral rights to the Big Viking and probably agreed to unfavorable terms; North Dakota farmers were unfamiliar with oil leases. But equipment problems and shaky finances doomed the project. The oil-drilling voyage of the Big Viking eventually ran aground. Today the state of North Dakota lists the well as dry and its final depth at forty-six hundred feet below the surface.

Playing his clarinet or his oboe at local festivities, maybe even oil well open houses, was something Dad would do later, but in 1930, he was only nine. His father took a new job at the lumberyard in Williston, a job that required bib overalls, not suits and touring cars, a step down for him.

But the scarcity of money during these years had an inversely rich influence on the two boys. They had a book, *Boy Mechanic: Projects for Boys* . . .

A big two-volume set, Uncle Rich inserts. *Walt and I inherited that from Vincent.*

. . . and they had an apparent knack for tinkering.

They built all sorts of things from scrounged stuff. Say you're a kid and you're inspired by Charles Lindbergh's transatlantic flight. You don't order a glider from the mail-order catalog. That would cost money. You build it yourself out of wooden laths and sheets. *We ran jumping down the alley with the bugger but couldn't do much gliding,* Dad wrote. *So I climbed on top of a garage with it. I leaped forward with my arms holding the glider up.*

And they built pushmobiles, whatever those were. *I can see all the working parts yet,* my father wrote. *How we scrounged for wheels and planks and axles and stuff. Our tools were meager and primitive. Rich and I built a complete touring car pushmobile, the enclosed body and doors made out of laths pilfered from a home construction site.*

As the family packed up and moved from house to house, the two boys likewise took things apart and then put them back together. Classic pre-nerd, pre-engineer behavior.

I'm feeling a little nostalgic for the generation of nerds, geeks, and engineers who found plenty of things to scrounge in those Depression years. Best not to get too nostalgic. Other things were in chronic short supply: widespread acceptance of farming techniques that would have helped hold the soil, knowledge of nutrition (both boys had plenty to eat but not always the right kind of food, and both suffered from malnutrition), and rain. In Dad's later years, his letters frequently opened with a weather report, more specifically a rain report. *We've had a couple showers recently but not nearly enough. It brings back terrible memories of North Dakota—year after year, the crops would be planted and we'd watch them wither. No wonder I like water. Midwesterners always tried to get into the Navy.*

Remainder of the 1930s

Wildcatters on the prowl for oil assembled, took apart, and reassembled drilling derrick after drilling derrick, poking holes in the ground all over western North Dakota.

Williams County attracted drillers more than most counties because of the Nesson Anticline. Another company set up operations in the same section of bluff country as the Big Viking, and the dusty eyes of North Dakotans turned hopefully, once again, toward the new enterprise.

Uncle Rich, left, and my father, inseparable boyhood companions, Devils Lake, North Dakota, around 1926. Family photo

Some people say the oil industry deliberately complicates and obfuscates the business of oil, all the better to control people and events. I wouldn't know, but when I find a typewritten well log of this 1937 well at the state archives in Bismarck, I sigh with pleasure. No legalese, no obfuscation. In a refreshingly straightforward way, the log writer recorded depths and types of rock encountered by the drill bit: clay, shale, sand, gypsum, dolomite, and on and on, drilling deeper and deeper into the earth's past.

10,201 feet: *Show Oil*

10,219 feet: *Good odor of oil*

10,281 feet: *drill pipe stuck on bottom 8/15/38*

Oh, that doesn't sound good. A writer for the Ray, North Dakota, *Pioneer* put it this way: *The drill bit "froze" and last week efforts to blast the pipe loose resulted in only about 7,000 feet of pipe being saved.* On and on, quite expensive . . . cost of pipe, leasing, surveys, etc., etc. . . . . end of project.

The drillers could have found oil in 1938, and maybe should have found oil. Pumpjacks today are pumping oil from nearby wells. But then there was the matter of the stuck drill pipe.

Throughout this same decade, my father's family's fortunes actually started to rise, and I'm damned ready for things to ease up. Oscar landed his steadiest job yet—business manager—at the new hospital in town.

Dad and Rich acquired a new baby brother—almost certainly an oops baby—who was born about a dozen years after they were. Maybe the new baby's parents coddled him because there was a little more money in the family's checking account; maybe his nature-nurture calculus was always skewed. Whatever the reason, Steve followed a much more troubled path than did his older brothers.

One last entry for the 1930s

As a boy and youth in Williston, my dad probably wasn't paying much attention to the growing pains of the fledgling oil industry, so he was spared the sting of disillusionment with that enterprise. But he felt his own brand of disillusionment in his small-town world.

His mother, inspired by her Lutheran upbringing, had imposed a strict moral code of behavior on her sons, and Oscar either endorsed that code or went along with it for the sake of family peace. After 1933—Prohibition was over—Oscar campaigned for local office on the wrong side of history. He was against liquor sales in beer taverns and against on/off sales in the town's beer taverns, according to Uncle Rich. Sounds like my grandfather was the antibooze candidate.

So when Dad saw his father enter a downtown Williston bar with his uncle . . . *That was shocking to him,* Uncle Rich says. Do as I say, not as I do. It's not the most effective teaching tool.

1940

You're the struggling North Dakota oil industry still searching for the pot of gold. What do you do?

You're a coming-of-age North Dakotan searching for your niche in life. What do you do?

The answer in each case is remarkably similar:

Get out of Dodge;

Explore here, explore there;

Set off a few explosives.

The Carter Oil Company drilled an oil and gas well nowhere near Williams County, the scene of the spectacular drilling failures of the previous decade. The well had an auspicious name, Exploration-North Dakota #1, but no production history, which means they came up empty, and today the well's status is officially "dry."

The same year, my father and his brother left their hometown for college at the opposite end of the state. In a family photo, they stand next to the Model T that their father had bought for them. They have the same apprehensive look on their faces they had when they were toddlers, peering around the corner. They both wear their new college sweaters and fedoras, and both of them hold their hands in front of them as if clasping sunglasses, but I doubt they had sunglasses. More likely they were snapping twigs or nervously twiddling their fingers. They look so alike, they could be twins.

My father should have started college a year earlier, but his parents hoped to save money on textbooks by sending the boys at the same time. Dad delivered groceries for a year in Williston, and then they both headed to the University of North Dakota in Grand Forks to major in chemical engineering.

Why didn't you want to work in the oil industry? I ask Rich.

It barely existed! Rich says. *In the '40s, it barely existed.*

They have already loaded the car with their meager belongings—you can see suitcases or boxes in the backseat. The trees in the background have leaves, but there are also leaves on the ground. Fall might come early to Williston given its location on the 48th parallel.

They posed for this picture, waved to their parents through the open windows of the car, and left home. They were pioneers in their own way. I know of no other direct-lineage Westbergs before them to aim for higher education.

1942

The Carter Company picked a completely different North Dakota county to drill in. The company probably drilled a number of test holes, set off explosives, and watched for signs of oil and gas in the reflected shock waves, a common practice then and now. They must have liked what they saw. Or maybe in 1942 they didn't really know what they were seeing.

They began drilling on June 8, 1942, and drilled almost nine thousand feet. The company reported to the state that it had drilled all the way down into the Precambrian. I'm not sure what the company had in mind. Oil drillers look for oil in sedimentary rocks, not in the planet's oldest metamorphic and igneous rocks. The well's status today? Dry.

The same year, my father and a few college friends spent an evening discovering what happens when you take theoretical knowledge and apply it in the field.

After the United States entered World War II, the military sent some of its fresh recruits to UND for specialized engineering classes, and as long as they were there, they might as well patrol the campus with wooden guns. Dad and a few classmates must have snickered at this faux military exercise. They also resented the recruits' presence because the new guys were getting all the girls, or at least that's the way my dad told the story.

If you're a bunch of chemical engineering students, talk turns quickly to the manufacture of homemade explosives. Nothing too sinister—toilet paper tubes filled with blasting powder, sealed on the ends and fuses attached—but at least one firecracker with real oomph.

In the spring of 1942, they unscrewed the fuses on the streetlights to achieve a more perfect darkness, then they spread out into the coulees and steam tunnels and on tops of the buildings, tossing toilet paper tube bombs and sending the wooden-gun guards scattering in all directions.

Remainder of the 1940s
The rocks beneath the state of North Dakota continued to stymie oil drillers. They dragged their oil-drilling equipment and crews from county to county. The list of counties they visited reads like a geography lesson for schoolchildren: Morton, Oliver, Emmons, Richland, Ward, Burleigh, Ramsey, Mercer, McLean, back to Emmons, Kidder. Today those wells are all dry.

During the same years, my father's wanderings took him far away from his home state. Along the way, he found a few things, lost a few things. In the lost column? Religion.

Uncle Rich, I say, *Dad always told us kids he had a rough childhood that he spent the rest of his life recovering from. Why did he say that?*

He was thinking too deeply! Rich says.

My uncle's assessment of how my dad went wrong makes me smile. Thinking too deeply is a bad thing?

Rich has told me in earlier conversations that when my father was a teenager in Williston, he started to read like a fiend and hang out with the town's free thinkers, code for non-religious people. And Meg had never allowed free thinkers into the house.

It made Walt miserable to go to church, get confirmed, stuff like that, Rich says. *As soon as we got away [from home], he was totally out of it. I was still in church in college, but he became anti-religious. That was the only area of disagreement between Walt and me,* Rich adds.

The two boys, joined at the hip by nature and necessity, had entered the centrifuge known as college and were beginning to separate.

Dad lost religion but, for the moment at least, found a future dictated by war. He and Rich joined the naval reserve and, after graduating, received instruction in radar at Cornell University, MIT, and Harvard. The educational tour took so long, the war was nearly over when they finally shipped out. No island combat for these two landlocked boys.

After the war and still searching (*with nothing better to do,* as Dad put it), my father hitchhiked to Colorado and enrolled in the engineering graduate school at the University of Colorado Boulder. But he must not have had the grad school fire in his belly, because when a friend wrote to him and suggested they hire on as crew with Merchant Marine ships and work their way around the world, Dad said yes.

First the free spirit friend had to pay off a few debts, so they delayed the start of their trip. The delay forced Dad into a serious exploration of the employment ads while he waited for his friend.

By the time my dad applied at the 3M Company in St. Paul, an inventive genius named Richard Drew had worked there almost a quarter century. In Drew's early years of tinkering—not always sanctioned by the folks who paid his salary—he invented products so ubiquitous today, you no longer think of them as inventions: masking tape and Scotch tape.

As an officer in the naval reserve, my father took radar and sonar classes at Harvard University in the 1940s. Walter Westberg

And with these inventions, Mr. Drew almost single-handedly transformed a sleepy sandpaper company into an innovation powerhouse. The company finally gave Drew his own lab, which he staffed with *eccentric underdogs* (in the words of a business reporter) and *a bunch of misfits—people who wouldn't fly in formation* (in the words of Art Fry, famous for his work on 3M's Post-it Note).

In 1947, Dick Drew's lab hired my dad.

I look back at this bit of serendipity and shake my head. I couldn't make up a more satisfying ending for a Depression-era prankster and incurable tinkerer like my dad. At the time, the lab was hot to trot to develop new products made of an experimental nonwoven fabric, and Dad jumped right into the mix.

Then, less than a year later, he jumped right out. He quit a job any self-respecting chemical engineer would kill for to work on a banana boat in Central America with his North Dakota friend. Part of me says, *What were you thinking, Dad?* And part of me says, *Go, Dad!* He was exploring, setting off small charges to measure what came back. He was only twenty-six. At the same age, I was married and had a steady job with the state of Minnesota.

I wince when I read his diary of his Panama Canal journeys. He recorded harsh assessments of humanity in general, women, blacks, and Latin Americans in particular. But he also showed a writer's inclination for reflection and navel examination: *What am I doing here? What have I done to get myself into this position?* And I wonder whether he had regrets over quitting the job.

Dad must have been receiving mail at the ports because he reported that *Pop is in full swing of harvesting. I hope this is his last season on the farm. He can be his own boss in other ways and, besides, he's wasting his talents out there.* My father makes this declaration—perched on a banana boat having just quit a great engineering job—without a trace of irony.

And his expectations upon returning to the workaday world were those of a cocky twenty-six-year-old engineering grad. He expected his 3M boss to hire him back, but the boss didn't. My mother has puzzled over this particular instance of Dad's unrealistic expectations. *When somebody has a good job and quits to work on a banana boat . . .* she says.

Dad took a job instead at a Minneapolis flour milling company. In his technical résumé, he says he did *process development, materials handling, milling instrumentation.* I'm sure it was a fine job, but what I remember him talking about later were the maggots. One of his tasks was to count maggot parts per unit of flour. There was apparently an acceptable level, and he had to make sure the company's flour didn't exceed it. Maybe that was the materials handling part of his job.

And what it meant for us kids later on was that we weren't allowed to eat a lot of raw cookie dough, even though it was just sitting there in the bowl and Mom's back was turned. He wanted those maggot parts to be cooked before we ate them. I remember swatting away my own kids when they tried to snitch from the bowl, and it wasn't just because I didn't want to go to all the effort of making cookie dough and not have any dough left for cookies. It was those maggot stories.

———

In a land far away, just east of Duncan, Oklahoma, the oil-drilling technique of injecting massive amounts of water into an oil well—hydraulic fracturing—achieved its first commercial success in 1949. But the domestic energy boom triggered by the combination of fracking and horizontal drilling was decades away.

———

By the end of this exploratory decade, both Dad and the North Dakota oil industry were *this* far away from, right on the *verge* of, finding their way in the world.

Perhaps my grandfather could feel success in the wind.

To help me understand what motivated Oscar—he is the reason my family has North Dakota mineral rights, after all—I try to figure out when he made his various land purchases. Aside from a lawyer's office, the first place to try to untangle the mysteries of land and oil is the Williams County Recorder's Office in Williston.

My apologies to Williams County residents, but their courthouse is pretty much ugly. Plain, practical—come on. They didn't think about architectural dignity or soaring vision when they designed it. Yes, it has a stone façade around the base of the building that looks like Morton gneiss, a classy Minnesota building stone, but even the gneiss can't class up this building. And inside it's the same plain Jane. Linoleum floors, Formica-topped tables, white walls, and fluorescent lighting.

But I soon detect a sense of humor or irreverence dressing up the plainness. The staff can not only find a parcel of land within seconds, but they can also tell out-of-town customers where the best lunch spots are. When they're not desperately busy, as they are most of the time, they banter about the early morning thunderstorm, the differences in over-the-counter painkillers or pedicures, and why men should be *made* to get pedicures. Handwritten signs tell visitors that if they change the settings on the public computers, somebody named Terri will break their fingers.

These people, by all rights, should be seriously grouchy—dealing with the intensity of an oil boom, all while working in an ugly building—but instead they are seriously laid back. Funny. They laugh if you laugh. If one staff person can't answer a question, another one jumps in. You get the sense these folks could possibly have fun together on sleepovers.

Many of their customers walk in here thinking about oil or oil-related projects. They're trying to find out who owns what land, who signed which lease, and which leases are about to expire. Many are on serious moneymaking missions, and they're so comfortable here, they wander into the staff areas. I can't always tell who is staff and who is customer.

Many years ago, my parents asked their longtime Williston lawyer to nail down Dad's mineral holdings and record them in one document. They had found this business of oil fairly confusing, too. That document now anchors my search. It has the legal descriptions of the parcels on which my dad was receiving oil royalties. We're talking township, range, and section, my favorite terms. Without these legal descriptions, your visit to the recorder's office becomes much more difficult, so difficult that you'd have to consider turning around and walking back out, after you've asked the staff for a recommendation of a good lunch place.

Even so, I stand almost clueless at the counter and wait for someone to show pity on me. Very soon, a young woman asks me what I need. I tell her, and she explains the process in crisp terms:

1. Go to the public computers in the back room and plug each legal description into the database to find out who owns the surface rights today. I learned early on that North Dakota allows the separation of "surface" rights from "mineral" rights. The land on which farmers raise crops is the surface; the minerals such as oil and gas are below the surface. In North Dakota, mineral rights trump surface rights. If you own the land and do not own the minerals below the surface, you are, for the most part, a bystander. You can't prevent a company from drilling on your land.

2. Go to the big filing cabinets behind the counter and look for those names on index cards. The cards, often several of them paper-clipped together, trace the history of surface ownership of that particular piece of land. The cards also record in which book and on which page the deed is located.

3. Once I know where the deed is recorded, I can go back to the public computers and search for it on the county recorder's database, or I can search in one of the big books itself.

It's an unforgivingly methodical process for a semi-organized, random-access thinker, and it takes me a while to get into a rhythm. I have to pester the young woman a few times.

A sign in the back room says, *Upstairs: we now have 15 public workstations: 9 in this vault; three in treasurer's vault; 5 in basement vault.* I make a mental note to check out the basement vault. I love the sound of that.

The upstairs vault is rimmed with shelves of enormous books labeled with such terms as *mineral deeds, miscellaneous deeds, ratifications Beaver Lodge Field, indexes.* There are two wooden tables where people spread out their stuff and open up the big books, but more often they stare at their laptops.

Slowly a picture of my grandfather's land purchases emerges, and Uncle Rich, who has never set foot in this office, has told me, *He did it all quietly.*

From what I know now of Oscar, he might have been a salesman, a guy with the gift of gab, but he was especially skilled at keeping quiet about certain things, and purchasing farmland was one of them. I finally find his first purchase, those 240 acres on the Nesson Anticline. He bought the land from Williams County in 1941 after someone else lost it for not paying the taxes. He was fifty-five years old.

This was less than twenty years after he'd been on the other end of a sheriff's auction, and as county treasurer, he had signed tax foreclosure documents, documents that slammed the door on people he must have known. He bought this foreclosed property after he'd been working at the hospital for several years and just after sending his two older sons off to college.

His first land purchase. That's the meat and potatoes. Now the gravy. What did he pay for this choice land? Here's what the deed says:

> . . . said County [that's Williams County] did on the 3rd day of April, 1941, sell said real estate to the party of the second part [that's Oscar] for the sum of Three Hundred Sixty and no/100 Dollars.

Oh my God—360 bucks? That's a buck fifty an acre, and that included the mineral rights. But wait—I should run the numbers through the inflation calculator. Today that amount would be the same as spending about $5,700, or about $24 per acre. Still impressive when you think how much North Dakota oil patch mineral rights must sell for today, if anyone ever sells them.

About six quiet purchases and ten years later, Oscar had bought 1,440 acres, not a lot by today's giant farm standards, but it must have felt positively feudal in the 1940s when the average North Dakota farm was about five hundred acres.

Oscar had learned his Depression lessons well. Owning that much land was all well and good, but he knew things could go to hell in a harrow pretty quickly. The documents contained in the databases and the hefty ledgers begin to tell the tale of methodical risk reduction:

Don't do this alone; take on partners.

It was a smart strategy, smart except for one thing, and you must know where I'm going with this. After oil was discovered, Oscar shared not only financial risk with his many partners but also the oil royalties.

Oscar! I want to shout as I uncover partner after partner in the old records. *Why did you do it? You—we!—could have made so much more money in royalties if you hadn't* . . .

My concentration breaks to take in the staff's discussion of the merits of spray-on tans. Maybe it helps take your mind off quitclaim deeds, whatever those are.

Time to step back. I realize I'm applying twenty-first-century horizontal drilling/hydraulic fracturing sensibilities to Oscar's 1940s life. Shouldn't do that.

Now for his first oil wells. Several were drilled shortly after oil was discovered in the state. My family signed a lease in 1957 allowing us to share in the proceeds of a 1955 well. This feels backward to me. Drill the well first, sign up the mineral owners later? I present this question to Jim, an acquaintance who works in the courthouse. He's lived here a long time and is a history buff. For clues to the answer, he sends me to the basement vault.

Is that where the good stuff is? I ask.

Jim has a delightfully wicked grin. He nods.

Look in the reception books, he says. People had to sign in when they wanted to record a document. *You can learn something about a case by seeing who showed up to record it.*

It's something. Maybe not much, but I love old documents, so I climb down the dark, narrow steps to that basement vault.

On the streets of Williston, the water trucks keep up a steady rumble, but down here in the courthouse dungeon, it's tomb quiet. I can hear when the exposed pipes gurgle, but they hardly ever gurgle. The walls are concrete blocks, but some of them are covered with brick, perhaps an effort on someone's part to class up the joint. It's a basement, a cluttered space filled with stacks of heavy books, filing cabinets, map cabinets, scraggly fake Christmas trees from celebrations long ago.

I sit at a long table surrounded by thick record books. Some are dated, some not. The only way to find what I want is to start lifting twenty-pound books off the shelves one at a time.

A man sits at one of the public computers nearby.

What brings you here? I ask. Cheeky question, but I was hoping I'd run into a landman, the person who rounds up mineral owners and gets them to sign leases. A lot of landmen come here to do title searches relating to oil. They're the ones who understand leases. I can't tell if he's a landman because I don't know what landmen usually look like. He is casually dressed, not sloppy but not business suit. Is his face a little tanned? Tanned by the Texas sun, perhaps? Middle aged, balding a little on top. He is probably at the height of his usefulness to his company, old enough to be experienced, not old enough to be slowing down.

Other people, nonlandmen, come here, too. People like me, people doing family histories, real estate people. The genealogy types usually betray themselves with their confused expressions as they stare into the computers. Landmen are rarely confused, I would guess.

It's been a while since I posed the question, so I'll repeat it to remind you:

What brings you here? I ask.

He pauses. *I could tell you, but then I'd have to kill you.*

I laugh. *Must be oil,* I say.

He laughs, too, but he doesn't say.

I keep pulling the heavy, canvas-covered books off the shelves. After a while, Mystery Man starts to leave.

Are you in the oil industry? I ask him.

He nods.

Do you understand leases?

He nods and says yes.

Do you have a second to answer a question?

Sure, he says.

OK. We're good. He's clearly not going to kill me. I tell him about the 1955 well and the 1957 lease.

He groans. *That would be a huge red flag to me if I were doing a title search on the property.*

Great, I say.

Back then, people were more willing to do business with a handshake, he says. *But it's such a risk to drill without legal permission. Back then, it would have cost hundreds of thousands of dollars to drill, and without legal permission?* He shakes his head.

The well is still producing, I tell him.

Oh, I'm not surprised, he says.

Then I point out that my family didn't even own the mineral rights on the land where the well was drilled. We owned the rights on land adjacent to the well.

This just deepens the mystery for me, but it makes the picture clearer to the landman. Oil companies often pool mineral owners together for efficiency's sake, a practice sanctioned by the state of North Dakota. *It gives the company a big working playground,* Mystery Man says. The company probably expanded the pool to include my family a couple years after the well was drilled.

We talk for a few minutes more, oil insider to oil insider, right? I thank him for his time, he heads back upstairs, and neither of us has revealed our name.

It's 4:30, and the recorder's office is about to close. I wander back to my hotel and flop on the bed, bone weary. This rare do-nothing moment doesn't last long.

I get up and start digging through the files that sprawl across the other bed in my hotel room and pull out an old newspaper article. "Major Companies Will Drill for Oil" screams the banner headline, and the subhead, "Nesson Structure Being Leased for Development." Strong hopes, fever interest, wildcat wells to be drilled in the spring . . . the anticipation leaps off the page in bold type. The story ran early in 1941, just a few months before Oscar bought land near the exploratory wells on the Nesson Anticline.

Both Uncle Rich and my mom say Oscar bought land to farm again, pure and simple. He loved to farm! He wanted to be his own boss! Yes, sure. But I think it was more than that.

I call Uncle Rich again with a more precise question. He thinks of the northern parcels as his dad's farm, so I ask my question in a different way: *Why did Oscar buy the two parcels south of Tioga, down by the Missouri River?* NOT *the farm north of Tioga,* I say.

Rich's answer is matter of fact, as though I've never asked a similar question. *Dad wanted to pretend he was a businessman, that he had a knowledge of the whole area. The original oil exploration of the Nesson Flats was nearby. He bought the land just to get in on something that might be developing.*

Well, all right then. One question down, a million to go.

Oscar wasn't the only Westberg who hoped to get in on something that might be developing. His grandparents had hoped to get in on the opportunities in the new world. His father had hoped to make his mark as a businessman on the frontier.

I had not known about this family thread. Do I have this thread? Should I want to get in on this new fracking-frenzy world?

My grandfather signed his first oil lease in 1950.

When two oil brokers finally talked to Oscar and Meg about doing business together, all four of them probably sat at the couple's dining room table—papers and maps scattered all over it—in their Williston home. Maybe they all had cups of coffee in front of them. My grandmother might have put out a plate of cookies.

Imagine how eager Oscar was. When he bought a couple

hundred acres on the anticline, this conversation was what Oscar had been anticipating. But oil leases were a novel concept to North Dakotans, and even if they hadn't been, critical thinking skills turn to mush at the prospect of making money.

Think how we buy lottery tickets today. We don't pause at the SuperAmerica checkout counter with a statistician or a calculator and work out the odds of winning, which are typically a jillion to one, while the customers behind us wait patiently. Instead it goes something like this:

Honey, this here is our ticket out of this dump.

Ka-ching! says the cash register.

The odds of finding oil in Williams County in 1950 might have been a little better, although I haven't put that question to a statistician.

But I do know that Oscar's first lease reads like a how-to on how not to write an oil lease. I pull up to a table in a Williston hotel room with my own cup of coffee and evaluate my grandfather's 1950 lease against today's contracts and today's advice.

The state of North Dakota's sample oil lease says the oil company gets five years to find oil.

In a publication aimed at contemporary mineral owners, a North Dakota economist offered this advice: *Try to keep the primary term as short as possible as this encourages earlier exploration. Considering the current situation, it would be unwise to sign a lease covering a period of more than five years.* By "current situation," he was referring to the success of hydraulic fracturing and horizontal drilling in bringing up oil from that dense North Dakota shale.

My grandparents agreed to let the oil company search for oil for ten years. Today with the oil patch in such hot demand, nobody would agree to ten years.

The North Dakota economist suggested that mineral owners limit the minerals they lease. Name them, specify them, and reserve the others for another lease later on. The state's sample oil lease does that.

My grandparents didn't do that. Whatsoever.

Mineral owners should limit the reasons an oil company can suspend operations and keep the lease active, the economist suggested. In other words, go for the Mini-Gulp.

My grandparents went for the Big Gulp list of reasons: acts of God, adverse field, weather, or market conditions, inability to obtain materials in the open market or transportation to it, war, strikes, lockouts, riots, or other conditions or circumstances not wholly controlled by lessee. This last reason— other conditions or circumstances—sounds roomy enough to drive several water trucks through.

Today, just about every well drilled in North Dakota produces oil. Oil companies are confident that their multimillion-dollar investment in the Williston Basin will pan out. They offer mineral owners royalty rates up to twenty percent of production.

My grandparents got twelve percent of the oil company's production, and of course, they shared that with a dozen other folks.

Then there's the Mother Hubbard clause. My effort to decipher my grandfather's first oil lease demands a rereading of a nursery rhyme and a brushing up on British history.

Once upon a time . . .

Britain's notorious King Henry the Eighth wanted out from his marriage to Catherine of Aragon. She wasn't producing a proper heir for him, and besides, he was madly in love with another woman, Anne Boleyn. He asked Catholic cardinal Thomas Wolsey to get down to Rome and convince the Catholic Church to grant a divorce, normally a no-no in Catholicism. In case you've forgotten the rhyme:

> Old Mother Hubbard went to her cupboard
> to get her poor dog a bone
> But when she came there, the cupboard was bare
> and so the poor dog had none.

And the translation: Cardinal Wolsey (Old Mother Hubbard) went to the church (the cupboard) to get his friend Henry (the dog) permission for a divorce (the bone), but as we all know, the church came up empty (the cupboard was bare).

In order to split from his wife, King Henry had to invent a whole new church, the Church of England.

The nursery rhyme's connection to these dusty historical events is disputed, but no matter. Oil and gas lawyers now use the term "Mother Hubbard" to describe a clause in which a mineral owner (often a farmer) bends over backward to please the mineral developer (an oil company) by allowing the developer to use property not specifically named in the lease.

The North Dakota economist told mineral owners no, no, no. Get rid of the clause. *Any mention of a Mother Hubbard clause or a cover-all clause should be deleted,* he advised. Back in my grandfather's day, I suspect nobody offered that advice, and Mother Hubbard and her cupboards are part of my grandparents' oil contract.

Is the moral of the story, "Don't sign an oil contract unless you can see sixty years into the future"? In Oscar and Meg's defense, what did they know of oil leases? What did anybody know? Nothing! But they were excited to *get in on something.*

True, all true. The hitch is this: if the oil company finds oil, and if the well keeps producing, even if it's paltry production, that oil lease remains valid. The sixty-plus-year-old lease that my grandparents signed in complete ignorance? My father inherited it from his father, my mother inherited it from my father, presumably someday my siblings and I will inherit it from my mother, and if I continue the pattern, my children would inherit it from me. If oil drillers are still pumping oil out of North Dakota by the mid-twenty-first century, my family could be staring glassy-eyed at the terms of a mid-twentieth-century oil lease. It's enough to make you want to hire a lawyer and sue somebody.

It's 1951 in the bluff country near the Missouri River, western North Dakota, and a crow soars over the bluffs. I ask this hypothetical crow a favor:

Please fly (as a crow would, of course) from the site of those early oil-drilling failures on the river bluffs to the farm about seven miles away where oil was finally discovered in commercial quantities on a fine spring evening in 1951. My crow agrees. Halfway in between, the bird flies over my grandfather Oscar's land.

North Dakota oil had finally come of age. Many celebratory beers must have been consumed that night and the next day, and many tales must have been spun. If my 1951 crow chills out at the farm where oil was discovered, roosts on the branch of a Juneberry bush, it will see one of these tales unfold.

Bill Shemorry, a news photographer for the *Williston Press-Graphic,* wrote in his book *Mud, Sweat and Oil* that his boss told him the evening of April 4, 1951, to put on his hip boots and get his butt out to a drilling site in the eastern part of Williams County. Word was they'd found oil. Shemorry had hip boots? Maybe he was a duck hunter; I don't know. The boots advisory had nothing to do with ducks and more to do with spring snowmelt. Water was everywhere, covering the fields and roads.

Shemorry said he could see the gas flare from miles away, and when he got closer, he had to drive past hundreds of spectators, drawn by the substantial flare. Photographers pay attention to light if nothing else—including simple hygiene and deadlines, in the case of some news photographers I've known—and this bright-as-day flare was just what Shemorry needed. It lit up Lake Snowmelt, and the windless night helped provide a glassy reflection of the drilling rig and gas flare.

He put on those hip boots and waded into the water with a tripod and his Speed Graphic camera, a camera that recorded images on four-inch-by-five-inch negatives. Huge negatives. High resolution. My father loved these large-format cameras, lugged them around whenever he went out shooting. Photographers today don't use these monsters to record car accidents and fires and wars, but if they've studied the history of their profession, they always speak in hushed tones about the old Speed Graphics and the photographers who used them.

Shemorry couldn't check the quality of his images on the spot the way we all do now with digital cameras and smartphones. Instead he took about a dozen shots, trusted his light meter, his camera settings, and his experience to give him the quality he wanted, and then took off.

North Dakota's first commercially successful oil well, the Clarence Iverson #1, is reflected in a slough by the light of a gas flare, south of Tioga, North Dakota, on April 4, 1951. The damage to the negative resulted, in part, from its heavy use at the state archives in Bismarck. William Shemorry/State Historical Society of North Dakota

He started driving to the printing plant in Minot on U.S. Highway 2, but remember, it's spring and there's water everywhere. *Near Lonetree, there was a stretch of road that was under water nearly the length of a football field . . . With vehicles ditched on both sides, at least I could tell where the road was supposed to be,* Shemorry wrote. He navigated a route halfway between flooded vehicles and somehow made it through the lake.

In Minot, he successfully developed his negatives and made prints, then raced triumphantly back to Williston, buying a six-pack of beer along the way, which may or may not be an apocryphal part of his tale. It goes down well, though, the part about the beer, and even the part about being stopped by a bored Stanley, North Dakota, police officer and Shemorry not wanting to stand too close for fear the cop would smell his beer breath.

His oil discovery photo appeared in North Dakota newspapers, of course, but also *Life* magazine and *U.S. News & World Report.*

At the state historical society, I ask the librarians if they have a print or a negative of Bill Shemorry's photo. After some searching, they find a few of the negatives, and I choose a damaged one for its ability to convey the decades-long journey from Shemorry's camera to a box in his basement to a climate-controlled library in Bismarck. In this shot, I imagine Bill Shemorry standing in the flooded field with his tripod and his hip boots. I don't know why he didn't choose this shot over the one that appeared in the *Williston Press-Graphic.* The reasons for that decision are lost. Shemorry died in 2004 in Williston.

———————

But what about my father? He had turned away from his Lutheran upbringing and away from his home state, although I suspect he faced North Dakota durum wheat day after day in his flour mill job.

Let's ask the crow to take another flight, this time all the way from the Tioga oil well to St. Paul—six hundred miles—to see how my father's doing in 1951.

The crow settles on a utility pole near downtown St. Paul where 3M has a lab and hears the good news: my dad's first boss at 3M has relented and hired him back after his dalliance with the banana shipping and flour milling industries. To be sure, Dad was hired to work in the Ribbon Lab, not the sexy Bohemian Lab run by 3M wunderkind Dick Drew. The Ribbon Lab sounds like a consolation prize, but my mother assures me it wasn't. It was in the Ribbon Lab that my father began a satisfying thirty-year career as an inventor, a professional tinkerer.

He must have heard about the discovery of oil in his home state as he was getting to know his new labmates and plunging into the new job. His father surely told him, or Dad read it in the newspapers. But he didn't remark on it in any of his journals, essays, or memoirs. He had moved on.

And my 1951 crow is morphing into a stork. My mother was pregnant with her second child. Me.

ASSIGNMENT

All provisions of this lease shall be binding on the heirs, successors, and assigns of the mineral developer and mineral owner.

An oil broker or oil company often assigns (sells) the agreement to another person or company, and the mineral owner assigns, or passes on, a lease to his or her heirs.

WILLIAMS COUNTY, NORTH DAKOTA

In the next few years, I was busy being a little kid and doing little kid things like eating caterpillars in our front yard (that's what I'm told), so I don't remember much of the following.

My grandfather, old enough to be retired, experienced a mild heart attack. The one thing you should do after you've had a brush with death and your family stands to inherit a lot of property is visit a lawyer and get your affairs in order. Oscar didn't do that; he did other things instead.

He wandered around the Midwest giving inspirational speeches for a beneficial society, Lutheran Brotherhood. He was still selling insurance for the group.

What were his speeches about? I ask Uncle Rich.

It was always the same, Rich says. *We're responsible to take care of the things that God gave us. His theme was always stewardship.*

Rich pauses and then adds, *And they always had a little humor in them.*

Smart, I say. *Get the audience on your side.*

He also got back into farming, thirty years after losing his Alamo homestead. He drew crop maps, ordered seed for his tenant farmer, and helped with the harvests. He began adding the sharp angles of machine sheds and granaries to his personal patch of the plains, and didn't leave the work to younger men. He got up on the roof with hammer and nails and even slid off a roof, scraping his back.

And he fiddled around with an idea for an invention. The world needed a clamp, he decided, something that would keep a power cord and an extension cord from parting company when you were in the middle of building, say, a machine shed. He asked my dad, a bright and shiny engineer newly reinstated in a research lab, for help in constructing models of this clamp and exploring the possibility of patenting his idea.

They were successful. Oscar was awarded U.S. Patent No. 2,720,633, which explains the rationale for the clamp in what I assume were my father's words:

It frequently happens that extension cords must be suspended from overhead appliances or outlets, moved about, pulled over and around obstructions, and generally subjected to stress during use.

So, Oscar was giving speeches, farming, building machine sheds, and inventing clamps; he also had the task of managing his brand-spankin'-new mineral rights. The 694th well to be drilled in North Dakota was drilled on his property in 1954. The company named it the Oscar E. Westberg #1. It's the well in the old photo I brought to my father when he was dying.

I know now that oil companies do sometimes name oil wells after landowners or mineral rights holders, and Bill Shemorry, the Williston news photographer, shot both the nighttime discovery of oil in North Dakota and my grandfather's first oil well.

A second oil company drilled another well on his property the following year, and just to make things really confusing for me, this well was named the O. E. Westberg #1. I have a copy of a check made out to Oscar. The check for $3,179, the equivalent of almost $28,000 today, probably represented Oscar's bonus for signing the lease authorizing his second well. A lot of money. Even three thousand would have been a lot.

He received the check in April; the well spudded—that is, the drilling began—in May.

Some of Oscar's bonus money might have gone immediately into long-distance phone calls to the oil companies after salty wastewater spilled from open pits onto twenty or thirty acres of his farm fields. The spill killed the crops, and for a while at least, nothing but thistles grew on those acres.

He was starting to make a little oil money, which makes it all the more bewildering to learn that Oscar and Meg sold a few of the mineral rights they had so recently acquired.

Why did they do that? I ask Uncle Rich.

I guess there was enough activity in the area, Rich says. *It brought the price (of mineral rights) up. And he probably needed the money to help Walt and me get through school.*

Then Rich veers off to indulge in a general gripe session about the oil industry of the 1950s.

You couldn't believe the promises of the oil companies because they made many promises that never came through. My dad signed leases, but the drilling seldom came through. I remember him saying, "Yeah, yeah, they're gonna drill six more wells in section so-and-so."

But in general, my grandfather was having a great time in the early 1950s. No wonder he didn't want to retire. Even a second heart attack and an extended stay in Arizona to recuperate didn't stop him from trying to drum up a little more oil activity. Three of his letters survive. That's it. Three.

We remember your courtesies, he wrote from Arizona to a small oil company based in Bismarck, *and your offer for minerals and I think you were very fair at that time, although we did not sell.* Brave of him to approach the company again after having turned it down once before. *In the event of a deal, when would you expect to commence drilling operations? You may write us here at Phoenix.*

The president of the company did indeed write back, assuring Oscar that his company wanted to do business, but they just weren't sure. At the end of the president's letter, he reported on the lackluster performance of nearby wells. A bargaining tactic, I suspect, to tamp down Oscar's expectations of a big bonus.

Oscar and Meg left Phoenix to visit us in St. Paul in the spring of 1956. I don't know why, maybe just to visit their son's growing family. My mother was pregnant with her fourth child, my youngest brother. Oscar told my sister and me bedtime stories one night. I remember liking my grandfather and laughing at his homespun tales. I was four, a great age for grandpas and stories.

He sure could make them up, Meg wrote to me later. *I had only one story Rich and your dad had to hear every night.*

Later that night, at age sixty-nine, my grandfather had his third and final heart attack, and he died the next day without a will.

At the time in North Dakota, if a husband died without a will, his wife and children split the estate in this way: one-third to the surviving spouse; two-thirds divided equally among the children. Over the years, Oscar's failure to write a will has fueled endless speculation, a family sport that continues today.

Did he do it on purpose? I ask Uncle Rich. *Not leave a will?*

I guess he felt that if he did leave a will, Rich says, *he'd have to leave everything to his wife, and he didn't trust women about financial things. She wrote all the checks for the household finances. He trusted her for things like that. That was natural in those days.*

Era-appropriate sexism aside, Oscar might have wanted to make certain his two older sons inherited part of his estate, including the potential for oil income. Meg had already exhibited a tendency to indulge her youngest son, Steve, who wasn't following his older brothers on their valedictorian/straight arrow/Eagle Scout path through life.

As for the lack of a will, I may as well contribute to the speculation: the most likely reason Oscar didn't leave a will is that he was too busy. He just never got around to writing one.

My grandparents on the left with two friends, my uncle Steve seated in front, Williston, 1940s. Walter Westberg

And because he didn't, Meg had to share his estate. If he had left everything to my grandmother, his estate—all of it—would most likely be in nonfamily hands today. Money had a way of flying from her hands to Steve's hands and from there into thin air. Because my grandfather didn't leave a will, my mother today receives oil checks.

Nobody in my family will ever solve the puzzle of Oscar's choice because this congenial talker kept quiet about it, as he did about so many other things.

———————

I leave Williston early on a Saturday morning to meet the farmer, Darren, who now owns my grandfather's surface rights on the land once known as Westberg Farms. I want to see this place that meant so much to Oscar, the land that freed him from the two old nurses at the hospital. I want to feel my grandfather's presence. Best way to get there is to head east on U.S. Highway 2. It's about a fifty-mile drive.

It's foggy, and construction narrows the road down to two lanes. I can't see the oncoming cars and trucks until they're right across from me. I slow down, but now I'm watching the clock, and I figure I didn't leave early enough.

Once again I juggle the tasks of map-checking and driving—maybe I should join the twenty-first century and get GPS—and because of the fog, I don't see my turn till the last second. It's a gravel road. I knew it would be gravel, but I forgot it would be all beat up because of the trucks. My car thumps in and out of potholes, and I slow down again, but after a while the potholes taper off, and I speed up.

I'm listening to Mark Knopfler and Dire Straits. This music became comfort music for me a few years ago when I was taking a grad-level course to learn how to teach English to adult non-native speakers. I would plunk it into the CD player on my way home to help me recover from standing in front of a classroom full of eager students with blank looks on their faces, each of them mystified by both the language and my lesson plan.

Mark Knopfler can't help me now, though.

My car starts slithering. It must be because the road is soggy from all the rain, I'm going too fast, and this car is slithery anyway, not a great road-gripper. Spoiler alert: I don't roll over in the ditch on this trip, and I don't plunge into a pothole and disappear, but the gravel road, supposedly a direct route to Darren's house, is definitely snickering at me the farther north I go.

The road turns left as if to detour through a little ghost town, foundations tilting, walls crumbling, then it straightens out and heads north again. Ten miles later, it turns left again for no apparent reason—just to be ornery, I think—and by now, I have to stop and look at the maps to make sure I'm still in an identifiable spot on the planet because the farm fields look the same from here to the horizon in all four directions. I worry that if my navigational concentration lapsed for even a second somewhere back there, I might be on the wrong gravel road. By now, I'm fifteen minutes late.

I call Darren and hope like mad I can get reception. I do, and what I really want to say is, *Darren! I'm so sorry, I don't even know you, but holy shit, what's up with this road?! Why does it keep turning left, and it's really soggy, and I thought it would be a straight shot north, and can I actually get there from here? But please don't ask me where* here *is because I'm not entirely sure.*

I don't say all that, but I come close. Darren, bless his heart, doesn't care that I am going to be late, but he does ask, *What are you doing on* that *road?* He advises me not to worry about the doglegs to the west, that the general tenor of the road is north, and I should stick with it. I don't remember whether he warned me about the lake.

Once again, I've mellowed out, and I'm doing Mark Knopfler's walk, the walk of life, when I approach the lake. The narrow gravel road turns into a causeway and goes right across the lake. I feel as though I'm channeling the photographer Bill Shemorry as he raced across the plains to develop his oil discovery negatives. I slow down again to run through my options:

Give up and turn around.

Check the map again.

Call Dave, but I might not get reception.

Cry.

Here's a chance to say I've been lucky enough to feel the thrill of travel. I've hiked up to the toe of a ferociously melting glacier in Alaska and smelled the sulfur fumes of an active vent on a Hawaiian volcano. I was knocked flat by a steady gale at the tip of South America, and I've canoed alongside a dog-paddling black bear in northern Minnesota. This solo slithering through a lake on the Great Plains? It's right up there.

You can imagine how good Darren and his wife, Joan, look,

all smiles and North Dakota friendly. They offer me a cup of coffee, but caffeine on the heels of driving through a lake doesn't seem necessary, so I decline.

Even though they must have a few other things to do, Darren and Joan take me on a tour of the land that my grandfather was so proud of. We ride in their big truck, a vehicle not fazed by car-eating puddles or lakes. People don't mess with small cars here, and if I lived here, I wouldn't, either.

Joan, who is driving, pulls in at each well pad to identify the well and allow me to take photos. *Is it OK to do this?* I ask. I'm thinking corporate America might not like this casual trespassing. They give me a quizzical look and continue to well pad hop.

These two North Dakota farmers have a solid case of the love-hate thing with the oil companies. The hate half: Darren says the companies need his permission to lay a pipeline for natural gas across his land, and they offer him a fee—thousands of dollars—for the privilege of doing so. But Darren says the companies don't always restore his property to its previous state, so he's grown skeptical of their promises. One of the companies didn't pack the dirt adequately after installing a pipeline near a well, he says, and while spraying his crops, his sprayer—with him on it—fell into the depression, causing $40,000 in damages.

We drive past the depression, and I can see it. The company built the pipeline for one of the wells that is now producing and paying royalties to my mother.

As we plow through puddles on the gravel roads and check out section after section, Darren strikes me as a levelheaded guy who isn't prone to exaggeration. He tells about a company that called to ask for pipeline access. Darren says he told the company's representative that if he saw him on his land, he'd shoot him, and I believe him. That's the hate part.

The love part: Darren's mother earns oil royalties, and she no doubt enjoys the money.

Joan turns down a dirt track that leads to the middle of a section. A utility line runs overhead, and wheat fields are on either side. Dragonflies, a few barn swallows, and the abandoned buildings of my grandfather's old farmstead populate a grove of trees. If a photo exists of this farmstead in its heyday, I've never seen it, and today is not its heyday.

Why are the buildings still here? I ask. They're clearly not usable.

I guess I don't know, Darren says. *They've always been there. I just never tore them down. Sometimes it's kind of nice,* he says,

The current owner of my grandfather's farm keeps old buildings on the site for a sense of history. Lisa Westberg Peters

to have the old buildings around. They get torn down and farmed around . . . There's no history.

Uncle Rich has told me about some of the history that now leans or lies flattened in the high grass. Oscar and his tenant farmer used boards from the original homestead's barn to build the machine shed over there. And that granary was built of war-surplus planks from the crates holding gliders for the invasion of Europe during World War II.

Professional scroungers. Today most of us have lost or never knew the art of scrounging.

The house was moved off the land by subsequent owners, but the basement is still here, filled with water. And there's an old water pump. I doubt it works, and even if it did, I'm not sure how good the water would be. Darren and Joan say they don't drink the local water. It's always been too high in iron and sodium.

Is this the homesteader's shack? The place where Meg wiped the sweat off her forehead to keep it from dripping in the stew? The building has collapsed to the extent it has nearly disappeared in the high grass, although the roof forms a solid triangle that rises bravely above the plane of grass. Behind the triangle of roof, a circular granary, a storage bin for the farm's wheat, offers functional and geometric contrast. In the far distance is another farmstead, another grove of trees, an oil well on the right.

I hesitate for only a second before pulling off a shard of brittle wood from the shack's roof—a tiny souvenir from a place Oscar loved—to take home to Minneapolis. The wood grain forms a graceful curve around a knot, and the growth of yellow and orange lichen follows the same swirl, obeying whatever rules of physics and biology are at work here.

I thought I would feel my grandfather's ghost here, but it's my father I feel. He would have loved to photograph this North Dakota still life, this splendor of weathered geometry. He wouldn't have asked me along on the photo shoot, but he would have invited me into the darkroom to see what he'd come up with.

I have a 1953 crop map that shows Oscar planted mostly wheat here and a little flax. He labeled a few areas prairie, which I suppose meant the ground hadn't yet been broken with the plow. Subsequent crop maps showed the presence of oil wells, but in 1953, there weren't any. Darren and Joan, and other farmers in the area today, plant wheat, but they also plant peas, lentils, canola, sunflowers, and soybeans.

Each year, Oscar and his business partner drove out from Williston to help with the harvest and . . .

. . . *their wives had to go out and cook,* Rich says. *It was primitive, primitive, primitive. Tarpaper-covered homestead shack, laths holding the tar paper on. It had a respectable kerosene stove that was used to heat the house and a little room off the back. They hired transients to help with the harvest. My mother hated it.*

I wouldn't like it, either. Late summer? Hot. And then you're standing in a shack, cooking potatoes and roast beef in a big Dutch oven on a kerosene stove. Good thing I didn't marry a guy who wanted to be a farmer.

I'm glad Oscar didn't leave a will. The family intrigue over Oscar's intent leaves no mark today in the farmstead's grove of trees. It does not wrinkle the air of this bright blue sky. This place is the definition of pastoral. I love it, and I will hate it when I have to leave.

Darren points out an antiquated combine tucked into a coulee. I had missed it entirely. It looks oddly like a praying mantis, waiting in a low spot for its next victim. When Oscar's estate was finally settled, among his personal property were two Chryslers (1947 and 1952 models—clearly he became a Chrysler man), shares of stock in the Williston Community Hotel Company, miscellaneous household goods, and farm machinery, of course, including an *old combine and tractor.* Maybe it was this same combine, rusty and insectlike, that today adds a little more iron to the soil.

Have you seen enough? Darren and Joan ask politely.

I nod, even though it's not possible for me to see enough. I don't know how to say that without sounding like a sentimental basket case.

Sure, I say.

The next day, the *Williston Herald* runs a front-page story about an accident that happened on U.S. Highway 2. The story begins:

> Three men were killed in a six-car accident near Stanley early Friday morning.

Only it wasn't cars. It was trucks. The accident story is punctuated with phrases that terrify me: *heavy fog, swerved right, struck the right side of the tanker.* One truck ran into another truck ran into another truck and so on until one of them ran into a tanker trailer carrying crude oil, which exploded and burned for five hours, shutting down the highway, a few miles from where I had been driving under the same foggy conditions.

ROYALTY CLAUSE

The mineral developer covenants and agrees to deliver to the credit of the mineral owner a specified fraction of all oil and gas produced and saved from the leased premises.

If the oil company finds and produces oil and gas, it shares a portion of the production revenues with the mineral owner.

HUDSON, WISCONSIN

To walk on the St. Croix River beach my family used to own—the place where I became an environmentalist—I now have to approach it from our neighbors' property. Sometimes I call ahead to ask if it's OK to tromp around; sometimes I don't because it's always OK. It's hard to find their footpath from the bluff top down through the woods to the beach, in part because they use this place so occasionally. Their family is now scattered across the country.

I used to race down our own zigzag path from bluff top to beach, grabbing the same spindly saplings each time. To us, this path felt like a magic passageway. Today I walk more slowly down our neighbor's path—gotta watch the knees, there's a rotted step, there's a slanted one.

At the bottom of the hill, I try to get my navigational bearings. I didn't know north from south when I was eight, and that gap of navigational data persists in my adult brain. I look straight across at the forested bluffs on the far side of the river and say:

I know that's Minnesota. And then I thrust out my right arm and say, *So that must be north.* I thrust out my left arm and say, *And that must be south.* But it never sinks in. I have to do the same thing every time I visit.

Our old beach is a few hundred feet up the shoreline. My parents bought this river property—just three acres, but nearly priceless today—for a few thousand dollars shortly after Oscar died. My father wrote to Rich and referred to it as his summer fairyland resort.

For the first few years, our family drove out from St. Paul to spend summer weekends on the river. We camped in a grassy meadow, a former cow pasture, and for sure we heard bears, which we scared off by banging frying pans. This may be one of those memories that nobody else in the family has, but I know there were bears.

We explored the woods, canoed along the shoreline, or camped under the stars, all with bare feet. And today I take off my shoes again to dig my toes in the warm sand.

My father has died; my eighty-nine-year-old mother has inherited his mineral rights. Eventually my siblings and I will inherit her rights, and that imagined headline still smirks with incongruity:

Environmentalist Rakes in ND Oil Profits

Maybe I should give the oil money away when it comes to me. Even Mom, who always had more of an environmental sense than Dad, calls it bad money, tainted by the stain of pollution.

But I'm not just a cheerleader for clean air and water. Now I know that my ancestors—immigrants and pioneers—followed hope and their hearts, risked everything, and sometimes lost everything to succeed on the plains that are producing great quantities of oil.

And even if I didn't know those things, I'm my father's daughter. I loved him, and he loved North Dakota oil.

I've pushed around enough sand.

We can move on.

1957

My father is named administrator of Oscar's estate.

Dad, who had said goodbye to North Dakota more than a decade earlier, said hello again. He was suddenly a wheat farmer and mineral rights owner. He found himself writing dozens of letters to, and receiving just as many from, the people of his home state.

The on-site farm manager reporting in: *This year's crops were poor due to excessive heat for about a three-week period in July and lack of moisture . . . According to local Experiment Station records, this year marked the fifth consecutive year of below normal rainfall and this exceeds the drought of the thirties.*

The family's Williston lawyer, serving as oil scout: *According to quite authentic information, Oil Company X will be drilling their next well in the very deepest formations in which they have a great deal of confidence . . . This information is being submitted to you so that if any sharks should come in and want to steal the property, you will have a little advance knowledge as to what the developments are in that vicinity.*

The State Land Department in Bismarck saying hello: *The above listed [farm] loan in the amount of $2400 was granted by this Department on the 28th day of September in the year 1944. The above loan was due on the first day of December 1956 . . . Please make arrangements to pay this loan in full.*

And an oil company, reporting progress or lack thereof: *The well you inquired about was completed several months ago, but is a weak well and we have been unable to make it flow. We have ordered a large pump for this well and hope to be able to place it in production in a few weeks.*

Dad sounded weary as he outlined the options for his fellow heirs, his mother and brothers: we can sell the whole farm, sell part of it, rent it out, sell to the tenant farmer, or what the heck, *plant eggplant and strawberries on alternate quarters and see what happens.*

Uncle Rich in response: *We prefer gooseberries.*

Dad was out of his league and sick of the whole business. *I wonder when I'm going to get a full night's sleep. All the problems have to be resolved at night.*

1959

An oil company drills a new well on Oscar's anticline parcel.

I try to reconcile two seemingly irreconcilable facts:

1. The oil company is paying my mother and my uncle royalties—precious little, to be sure—on that 1959 well and a few more old wells.

2. And yet, on the state of North Dakota's website, the old wells on Oscar's anticline property were abandoned several decades ago. The pumpjacks should be quiet, not moving up and down.

I worry that I might have this wrong, that I've misidentified the wells.

Maybe Uncle Rich can help me. Oil companies assign numbers to wells, but the state of North Dakota uses different numbers. If you're lucky, you can identify the wells by their names, but the names of several wells might be very similar, and you don't want to get it wrong.

Rich, can you do me a favor? I ask.

Sure, he says.

I ask him if he would please call this particular oil company and get the state of North Dakota's identifying numbers for each well listed on the royalty statement.

They'll give the information to you because you're a mineral owner, I say to Rich. *Are you OK with this?*

Sure, he says. He takes down the phone number and says he'll get back to me. And he does.

She said to check the state's website.

Sigh. *OK,* I say.

But why don't you call her right now? he suggests. *I just hung up with her.* He gives me his owner number, and I call the oil company.

The person who just talked to Uncle Rich answers the phone. Already I feel as though the stars and planets are about to line up. I explain to her who I am, that I'm trying to help my uncle update his records. I want to square the wells listed on my uncle's royalty statements with the wells I see listed on the state's website. Can she please help me?

She starts down the list of eight wells that I assume are producing oil because they're paying my uncle and my mother royalties, albeit teeny-tiny amounts. She tells me the state's identifying number for the first well on the list and then the next one. And then she stops, stammers, seems confused.

These wells are plugged and abandoned, she says. The phrase "plugged and abandoned" is one of the more transparent oil industry terms. It means what it says: the well has been plugged with a series of cement plugs and abandoned by oil and gas drillers, at least temporarily. For whatever reason, the driller deemed the well unprofitable or otherwise a bad idea.

I can feel the oil company woman starting to pull away from the phone conversation. She doesn't give me the state's numbers for the rest of the wells, and when I ask if she or someone else with the company can take a further look and clarify this confusing situation—an oil company paying on plugged and abandoned wells—she says, *We don't have people to do that kind of work for our owners.*

They don't? That doesn't sound like great customer service. After we hang up, I send the company an e-mail request for the same information.

I don't hear back.

So I call the state of North Dakota. *Why are my mother and uncle making a few bucks off these abandoned wells?*

Here's what they tell me:

The oil company that developed Oscar's mineral rights on his choice Nesson Anticline land in the 1950s and 1960s pooled the mineral rights owners in this area into one big group. To keep Oscar's sixty-year-old lease active, this company need only maintain minimal drilling activity somewhere, anywhere, who knows where, within this big working playground, which is about eight miles long and three miles wide. To help you out, a comparison is in order. The island of Manhattan is longer and skinnier, but it also occupies twenty-four square miles.

All those mineral rights owners now split the tiny royalties generated by the company's minimal activity. It amounts to peanuts. The oil company, meanwhile, focuses its attention elsewhere, in areas where more recently drafted leases are in danger of expiring.

Put another way, the oil company can hang onto all those old leases with one finger.

But here's the clincher. In one of those quirks of oil industry fate, drillers don't salivate for the Nesson Anticline anymore. Fracking and horizontal drilling render the legendary upside-down canoe nearly obsolete. Today we don't need to search for the domed layers of rock that block oil from its upward migration. With unconventional technology, we head straight for the source rocks, the deep layers of tight shale where the oil remained locked up until now.

Oscar's quiet efforts to get in on something that might be developing? That plan worked for a few years, but that's about it. Today the parcels he bought for the sheer joy of farming generate far more oil income.

1960

My father builds a summer cabin in Wisconsin.

Eventually my father bought the lumber, nails, and tools he needed to build a summer cabin. He designed a lopsided or, as he put it, modified A-frame cabin with a sleeping loft in the peak of that leaning A and a porch across the front with a great view of the river valley. At night, we four kids would climb a ladder into the loft and from our cots listen to broadcasts of the Minnesota Twins baseball games on WCCO radio. Many times I've wondered how I got so lucky to spend a wild childhood on this river.

From my spot on the beach, I can see our old path up the bluff even though it's overgrown and strewn with logs and leaves. I start to climb the path. Maybe the new owners are trying to prevent the erosion we caused with our repeated and reckless journeys down the hillside. Columbines grew in this shady spot at the base of the hill, and it's where I first identified them. Horsetails, too, with their segmented stems. We pulled the segments apart and put them back together again, idle summer exploration. For all I know, they're endangered. We never thought about it. There were some right here, some a little farther up.

Wild asparagus grew in these woods. My mother helped us look for the tender spears in the spring, but sometimes we

My siblings and I exhibit a wide range of footwear in the loft of our summer cabin on the St. Croix River, Hudson, Wisconsin, early 1960s. I'm second from right. Walter Westberg

were too late, and the asparagus had already gone to seed. I liked the tickly feel of the lacy fronds.

I learned to love oak trees. Dad fretted about losing the oaks to oak wilt, so I fretted, too. I walked around with him, checking the leaves on the trees. One of the cabin's support posts rested on the stump of a bur oak tree. All summer, I collected and pressed oak and other trees' leaves in heavy books and then forgot about them, years later discovering them brittle.

I didn't just learn the names of the plants and birds that lived in the St. Croix valley. I came to need them. When Dave and I moved away from the Midwest in the early years of our marriage, I found that I could probably live without oak trees and cardinals, but why would I want to?

Looks like the current owners of the land have fixed up my father's A-frame cabin. It has a new roof and cedar paneling inside, and the rotted stairs to the beach path are gone, but it's the same cabin, the same shape, the same arrangement of rooms.

I climb back down the bluff to sit on the beach again. I used to bring a notebook down here, hide in the trees, and write *en plein air*. I wrote long poems, and over the years, I've run across rambly stories I sent to my grandmother Meg. She thought they were great. Now I pull out a laptop and tap these words onto the keyboard. I secretly hope Dave won't learn that I fired up this sensitive electronic device while sitting in the sand. It's the beach version of sitting in bed and eating toast while you watch TV; you can't ever, ever keep at least a few crumbs from landing in the sheets.

The frac sand mine I visited near Grantsburg, Wisconsin, is about seventy miles north of here. The oil and gas industry won't want the sand on this beach unless the rules and needs of the fracturing process change dramatically. The sand here is a fruit-basket-upset mix of grain size, shape, and mineral composition. Oil drillers want all smooth, all round, all quartz.

I carefully set the laptop on the beach, my rain jacket the only thing that separates it from the sand, and it takes me just a few seconds to find a Lake Superior agate along the shoreline, which is where we used to look for them. We collected buckets of them. We never bothered to collect the flat skipping stones that litter this beach. Those went straight into the river for rock-skipping contests. Dad was the best rock skipper, but my youngest brother might take issue with that.

A big boat passes, close enough for me to see the man driving it, and he's probably wondering who the hell I am.

It was from this beach that we loaded up Dad's homemade sailboat—the one he began building in our St. Paul basement—with sleeping bags, food, kids, and a Labrador dog, and off we went, tacking into the wind. Not only did the bathtub-shaped boat float, but we also managed to sail it to an island several miles upstream, where we camped for the night. And then we sailed back the next day. It was one of those family excursions launched on faith and peanut butter sandwiches.

I don't try to re-create the feel of my childhood when I come here. How could I? Too much time has passed—my parents sold the property right after Dave and I got married—and once again, I'm just a trespasser. I'm always aware that a bewildered or angry person might appear and ask me what I'm doing. I could call my whole journey back and forth across the Midwest *Trespass* because I've done so much of that as I wander into unfamiliar territory, trying to make sense of the way innovative drilling technologies have opened up not only oil-rich formations but questions and dilemmas for me.

My father gave me this summer fairyland resort and turned me into someone who loves the outdoors. My dad helped turn me into an environmentalist. What I didn't know was that he had sold forty acres of North Dakota mineral rights to help pay for the lumber and nails that went into the new cabin. He used oil revenue. I didn't know it when I was a kid. I do know it now.

Irony mews like a kitten when it's the subject of an academic exercise. Irony aimed at yourself has claws. It reaches out like a helping hand, but when you grab hold, you get poked.

Somebody should write it up: river paradise a gift of the unparadisiacal business of fossil fuel extraction, a gift from the guy who loved North Dakota oil checks.

All these years I felt lucky for my summers on a river, but I see now how luck wasn't much involved.

1962

My father is awarded his first patent.

In the summers, Dad commuted to work from the cabin, and once he got to the Ribbon Lab, he worked on ways to make better ribbon, but his lab got swept up in 3M's innovative frenzy with something called nonwoven fiber technology.

Years later, the *Minneapolis Star* ran a story about this inventive chain of what-ifs. One researcher figured out a way to shape the nonwoven fibers into a three-dimensional object, the article said. Then the Ribbon Lab *decided to use the process to make nonwoven brassiere cups,* according to the article.

You never know what you'll work on in a ribbon lab! The newspaper article didn't mention my dad, but his name is on the patent as co-inventor of that ill-fated brassiere. It was the first of his seven patents, and he received it about a decade after he shepherded his own father through the patent process. Dad used to chuckle about the brassiere, and good thing, because the bra was a bust, so to speak. The company supposedly tried it out on twenty volunteers, and nobody liked it. My mother claims she never tried it.

The idea of molding this nonwoven fabric into three-dimensional articles, though, found ample and profitable expression in other products, mostly in disposable face masks, which were so successful, it's always startling for me to see a photo of someone wearing a face mask other than a 3M mask.

The innovation engine was humming. *I suppose it was inev-*

itable, Dad wrote, *that, since we worked and lived in Minnesota, someone would suggest making a mask for protection against cold weather.*

My father's cold weather mask was reusable, heavier, and more durable than the previous dust and surgical masks. Dad described how he put on a prototype of the mask and ran up and down the alley behind his St. Paul lab in the middle of the winter. It sounded eerily similar to his description of running up and down the alleys in Williston to get a glider off the ground. The mask conserved the heat of his breath, he wrote, but some of the heat leaked out in the nose area and fogged his glasses, so he and his co-inventor went back to the drawing board.

He was an inventive guy, says Uncle Rich in frank admiration.

He was, but Dad was also practical. He chose to be inventive inside the corporate womb where many ideas for new products start with the marketing department. This choice landed him neither fame nor wealth, but it did pay him a steady salary for groceries and mortgages.

If my dad were a young staff scientist today, what would the marketing department ask of him? When I search for "3M green technology," I get whole pages of products designed to help customers *achieve sustainability goals—whether they are saving energy, reducing greenhouse gas emissions, or purchasing products that are made with fewer solvents.*

Maybe today my dad would be working on ways to make hydraulic fracturing less water- or chemical-intensive, or internal combustion engines more fuel efficient. Back in his day, somebody wanted a cold weather mask, and he invented one.

Dad came home at night and often told us about his projects in the lab. I don't know why I didn't catch the inventive bug from him. None of us did. We hadn't tinkered and scrounged our way through childhood the way he did. Instead I was learning that I enjoyed tinkering with words on a page. I wasn't yet dreaming of being a writer, but I had started to realize that writing was the same as thinking. I announced this observation to Dad once—in the car, of course, where all meaningful conversation between parents and offspring occurs—and he seemed awed by my youthful glimmer of wisdom. This surprised me because Dad was my hero. It was a little scary to think he might admire me.

1966

My father teaches me how to drive.

In North Dakota, grasshoppers chewed up the crops, oil well operators accidentally spilled saltwater and rendered patches of Westberg Farms unusable, oil leases expired, and new ones were drafted. I paid no attention to any of these goings-on. I was more interested in getting my license, and my father helped me enter the all-American world of driving.

The summer I was fifteen, Dad took me out on County Road F in western Wisconsin for some practice driving. I wasn't very good, but gimme a break; I was learning on a stick shift in a boxy Volkswagen bus. My father never lost his composure, not even when I shifted into the wrong gear and the error produced an expensive, scraping sound from the transmission.

1968

It's the '60s. I start paying attention, for God's sake.

After visiting our old beach and cabin, I drive several miles north, cross the river back to Minnesota, and continue heading north. I pull in at the Sunnyside Marina, which is sandwiched between two river crossings. About a mile upstream is a historic—read ancient—lift bridge, and just downstream is the site of a new freeway bridge meant to replace it.

"Just downstream" is an exaggeration. It would be more accurate to say the new bridge site is right on top of the marina. The construction cranes are so close to Sunnyside's boat slips, I can hear the workers shout to each other over the hum of the machinery.

This new river crossing, which will stretch from bluff top to bluff top like a concrete banner, is a far cry from the raft powered by mules that took my immigrant ancestors across the Mississippi a hundred and fifty years ago. It's also a generation or so bigger, higher, and faster than the two-lane highway bridge my family drove across this river in the 1960s.

Just beyond the new bridge site, the smokestack of a coal-fired power plant peeks out from the trees on the river's bluff. A river neighbor of ours fought hard to keep this power plant off the St. Croix, but sensing defeat, he argued just as hard for cooling towers to mitigate the impact of the plant's warm wastewater on the river's cool, spring-fed water and fisheries.

A high school student at the time, I was too busy studying the available guys and pretending to understand chemistry to get involved, but I was emerging from my childhood fog. I saw our neighbor lose the power plant battle and then win the battle for cooling towers. I watched this local controversy over industrial pollution gain national traction. Our neighbor's fight helped pass the National Wild and Scenic Rivers Act in 1968, a federal law that forbade major new public works from being built on protected rivers, including the St. Croix.

Except for this freeway bridge. Congress recently passed an exemption to the law to allow the construction of the bridge. I was furious at the time, but as I sit on the boat slip and watch the construction cranes sway like swans, I wonder what makes me so special. It's all right for my family to scoot out to a fairyland resort on cheap gas and frolic on the beach all summer, but now that we've had our fun, it's not all right for anybody else?

It's the same discomfort I am starting to feel when environmentalists frown on fracking but smile as they board fossil-fueled airplanes for discretionary trips. *We've been invited to a dinner in California. We're going to hike in the Italian Alps. Visiting our son in Norway . . . Japan . . . fill in the blank.* I've been a gas-guzzling traveler, too, but more and more I

Even after I left for college, I often spent time on my parents' property overlooking the majestic St. Croix River valley, Hudson, Wisconsin.
Stephen Cotter

see the hypocrisy. We can't make the connection? If we keep demanding the oil, someone else will happily fracture shale to supply it.

1971

I become a Swedish American hippie freak protester.

> On April 24, the Student Mobilization Committee to End the War and the National Peace Action Coalition sponsored a peace rally in Washington, D.C. Reports of the crowd ran from 200,000 to 500,000, depending on which "side" gave the estimate.
>
> *STUDENT VOICE*, WISCONSIN STATE UNIVERSITY–
> RIVER FALLS, APRIL 26, 1971

The student newspaper's managing editor traveled to Washington, DC, to report on the rally. He drove a beat-up van with six others.

I was nineteen, and I was in that van.

I keep telling my daughters I was a crazy hippie back in my college days. *We all were!* I say. The girls just laugh. *No, really!* I say. And they laugh again.

But I was. I attended antiwar rallies and marches at two universities, the University of Minnesota and Wisconsin State University–River Falls. I skipped classes because of the rallies. I had to withdraw from courses because I'd skipped so many classes. I quit school. I enrolled again. I shuffled around in beads and bell-bottoms. I knocked on doors with my boyfriend. I attended the first Earth Day celebrations and signed petitions against air and water pollution. I drank Boone's Farm wine. I ate marijuana brownies and then went swimming, an experience that taught me the value of being in complete control of my faculties when there's a choice of things to breathe—air or water. I frolicked in the buff at a friend's Wisconsin farm, never dreaming that someday, somebody would invent a devastatingly efficient way to transmit photos around the globe. And I climbed into an old yellow van for a peace rally in Washington in 1971.

I write to my old friend, the managing editor of the student newspaper, who is now hidden away in the Florida Keys, to ask him about the trip.

He speaks with pride about that van. *It was paneled with mobile-home walnut and three-inch-thick upholstery foam topped with basic carpet on the floor in back,* NOT *a sleazeball's cheap mattress. This was good stuff. I added a couch later.*

There was a curtain separating the driver's compartment to ensure privacy, he writes. *Lisa huddled in one corner. Everything was proper. The tires were good and the brakes were fair. There was a radiator problem, and we had a few stops.*

I'll say. I remember standing by the side of the van waiting, the hood up, my friend's head inside.

And I remember a semi somewhere in the Appalachians. We were heading down the mountain—along with all the other protesters from across the country—and the truck was right

Vietnam War protesters at a Washington, DC, rally I attended in April 1971. Stephen Cotter

on the van's tail. Anybody in the van who had been asleep on that three-inch foam was now awake. My friend attaches innocence to the driver's motivations, says that the guy's brakes were suffering on the long descent. Mountain routes have runaway truck ramps for such situations. But I remember somebody pointing a long camera lens out the back window of the van at the semi's license plate, and the trucker backing off. We all cheered. Hippie freaks 1. Redneck truck driver 0.

As I say, it was a crazy time.

I ask my friend, *Was I a freak back then?*

He laughs. *A freak? No. You're a Swede!* As if that explains everything.

Naturally, there's a YouTube video of this 1971 peace rally, the Vietnam War Out Now Rally, one of Washington's largest gatherings, according to the National Park Service. John Kerry spoke. He had lots of hair then, too. It was darker, but he had the same nose, same chin. I probably was too far away at the time to hear what he had to say.

1972

My father sells the land known as Westberg Farms.

All the political bubbling and boiling had no effect on the vast pools of oil hidden two miles beneath western North Dakota. It mostly just sat there, difficult and expensive to extract with conventional vertical drilling. The second oil boom, triggered by high gasoline prices and geopolitical turmoil, was right around the corner.

An oil company with a lackluster well on the Westberg Farms offered my family a fresh lease so it could drill a new well. My family balked at the company's offer and asked for more money. The oil company said, *Fine. You don't like our offer, we'll just keep that old, crappy well alive—barely—and your old lease will remain valid . . . forever.* The family signed.

My father, his brothers, and his mother finally sold Oscar's land—the surface rights—but retained the mineral rights.

Why did you sell the farm? I ask Rich.

Walt and Mom wanted to sell, and Steve had to sell, he says. *But the year we sold was a bad year. Just a year later, farm prices were much higher.*

My father might have wanted the money from the sale of the farmland, but he was no doubt sick to death of being an absentee farmer and worrying about wheat prices and hail damage. He had four kids, two in college, and by then, he and Mom had built a year-round home on the St. Croix. They were distracted.

Why didn't you sell the mineral rights, too, I ask Rich, *if you thought the oil wasn't going to amount to much?*

Gosh, no, Rich says. *It was a few thousand dollars a year, all gravy. We couldn't count on it, but we had thoughts that it might develop into something big.*

Sounds like Oscar. The hope for something big didn't keep my grandmother and her son, Steve, from selling their share of mineral rights—a few acres here, a few acres there—over the next several years. Meg's cash went straight to Steve.

1974

I graduate from journalism school.

My transcript was a neat, handwritten display of several letters of the alphabet including three Ws for withdrawals and a few Cs, one for tennis. I was no good at tennis.

The university didn't hold graduation ceremonies in the winter, so I immediately headed west with a tall, skinny guy named Dave to visit his brother in California. We drove Dave's old Dodge and got stuck behind a snowplow in Wyoming somewhere west of Lusk. When we tried to pass the plow on the two-lane road, the driver's blade flipped and dumped several tons of slush onto our windshield. This instant blindness forced us to slow down substantially, so it's even more miraculous we didn't die before the old car's wipers, grinding and groaning, finally slid the slush off the windshield, allowing us to see the oncoming car and swerve back to the westbound lane.

It was the first of many trips across the American plains.

REWORKING OPERATIONS

> During the primary term, if prior to discovery of
> oil and/or gas on the leased premises, the mineral
> developer should drill a dry hole or holes there-
> on, or if after discovery of oil and/or gas the pro-
> duction thereof should cease from any cause, this
> lease shall not terminate if the mineral developer
> commences additional drilling or reworking oper-
> ations within sixty days thereafter . . .

> *If the oil company doesn't find oil in the primary
> term, language like this gives the company more time
> to develop the property, and it keeps the agreement
> between mineral developer and mineral owner alive for
> a specified period of time. This clause is also referred
> to as continuous operations.*

HUDSON, WISCONSIN

What a difference cheap fossil fuel, a few social revolutions,
and modern medicine can make. My entry into adulthood bore
little resemblance to that of my Swedish ancestors a hundred
and fifty years ago:

Johannes and Inge were married in a state-sponsored
church. Their guests probably walked or buggied to the
ceremony.

Dave and I were married on the bluffs of the St. Croix River.
The sun lit up my straw hat and Dave's anxious face. Our
guests came from near and far by plane and car. They included
our families, friends, my grandmother Meg, and (courtesy of
my brother's brass quintet) the many voices of a Bach fugue
chasing each other beneath the blue dome of our sanctuary.

Johannes and Inge started cranking out the kids right away.
We did not, thanks to the pill.

We found jobs at a central Minnesota newspaper and dal-

Dave and I just before our wedding ceremony at the St. Croix River, 1975. Robert Peters

lied about childless for several years. Then the desire for children hit me with the force of a runaway double stroller.

When you have a choice about making babies, you also have the luxury of wondering whether you can afford them. Dave took a little time to crunch numbers in his head, but I was already picturing myself in a sunbonnet pushing the world's most beautiful and well-behaved baby in a perambulator, my biological clock ticking in the background.

My great-great-grandmother Inge died in childbirth.

I never once worried that I would die in childbirth, and of course, I didn't even come close to dying, although I wanted to die several hours into the wild-eyed panting part, no sign of baby and starting to get pissed off at birth coach husband and whoever else made the mistake of entering the hospital room.

Nine hours, countless trained medical personnel, and one blessed muscle relaxant later, our first daughter, Emily, was born.

Children, of course, turn those Victorian bonnet images inside out. For one thing, our daughter was far too small a human being to be held by an amateur like me. Why wasn't the hospital staff alarmed at this five-plus-pound sack of flour? Had she blinded them with her downy face and tiny nose?

When I went into labor two years later with our second daughter, Dave and I both felt as though we were pros. No sweat. My parents stayed with Emily, and we drove the five miles to our downtown Seattle hospital.

But it had snowed earlier that night. Seattle, an intensely evergreened city, doesn't plow. Why bother? they say. It will just melt. This policy might work if it weren't for all those steep hills. We started up one of those hills to the hospital and began to skid. Veterans of years of Minnesota winter driving, we barely noticed. *We can get up this hill,* we said. But apparently not in a rear-wheel-drive station wagon.

So, at about three in the morning, we parked the car several blocks from the hospital and hiked. Every once in a while, we'd stop for a contraction. I remember wondering, *How much crime might there be around here? Will a mugger even want to mess with a woman in labor? I think not, and besides, here is another contraction I have to focus on.* Whatever number my cervix was dilated to at the bottom of the hill must have climbed at the same pace we did.

You walked? the admitting nurse said. She about smacked her lips. *Oh, you'll go fast!*

And she was right. The midwife barely made it in time for Anna, another beautiful daughter, this one with a round face, her dad's dark hair, and, thank goodness, a few more pounds.

After each birth, those same highly trained medical personnel taught me a low-tech way to feed a baby. I was too busy trying to get it right to reflect on why nursing a baby is such a powerful experience. But one reason has to be its ability to close the gap between our ancestors—not to mention all of humanity—and ourselves. For a hundred and fifty years—a hundred fifty thousand years—mothers have nurtured babies the same way—baby to breast. Period.

Except for five years in the Seattle drizzle in the 1980s, I have lived and worked continuously in the Midwest, the land of my Swedish ancestors. And my daughters returned to the Midwest from colleges on the West Coast, got married, and are now pregnant with their first babies. They already have benefited from more sophisticated technology than was available to me. But they, too, plan to nurture their babies in this time-honored, but not time-worn, way.

And what a difference nature and nurture can make. In the 1970s and 1980s, the beneficiaries of Oscar's mineral rights managed those rights in wildly different ways during North Dakota's second oil boom.

My grandmother Meg was raised like a queen in a prominent Williston family. She alternately bragged about her successful negotiations of a new oil lease and fretted she was getting screwed by the oil companies. She constantly harangued Dad to stir up more leasing interest from the oil brokers, get some new wells, and rework the old ones, but she only sporadically apprised him of the fact that she was selling her mineral rights and passing on the proceeds to her youngest son, Steve, now married, raising four children, and perpetually out of money. In her final years, she gave almost everything she had to Steve.

This woman who had so many unrealized visions of musical grandeur and enough talent to support such visions, who had railed against booze and cards during my father's childhood, who later on taught card games to her grandchildren and sipped Mogen David wine, who had carried herself like royalty, this woman in her last years had to rely on the largesse of California taxpayers for her food and housing. My grand-mother Magna Diderikke Monson Westberg died in California at age ninety-four.

My father, on the other hand, probably had an overdevel-oped sense of responsibility. He was expected to understand the demands of being both poor and an Eagle Scout. Through the North Dakota oil industry's booms and busts, he held on to the vast majority of his mineral rights. He never expected much from North Dakota oil, but he also never stopped try-ing to drum something up. After high gasoline prices in the mid-1970s encouraged drillers to give those oil formations another chance, Dad sent letter after letter to landmen and oil companies:

> Dear Sirs:
> My brother, Richard Westberg, and I own mineral rights in the above parcel in Williams County. Our lease expires in August. It is currently leased to so-and-so.
> I would be pleased to consider any offer you feel you can make, especially one resulting in some drilling.

He even suggests which driller the oil broker could ap-proach because that company had earlier drilled on this parcel and brought in a successful well and *happiness to me.*

He sent a dozen letters suggesting drilling action a couple years after gasoline prices had peaked and were falling like a rock. It's easy now, from the safe remove of twenty years, to prop my feet up on the coffee table and say, *A little late, Dad!* What oil company would want to rework a failed well, and what oil broker is going to renew an expired lease now that oil prices are headed in the wrong direction?

A year later, when oil prices remained relatively low, Dad wrote:

Can you believe the oil price news? I can see how easy it would be to get corrupted and try to influence things your way if most of your income depended upon high oil prices.

He was always trying to get some balls in the air, but even college-educated mineral rights owners couldn't always fathom the mysteries of the oil industry.

Oil companies occasionally didn't pay enough; he had to write them a letter asking why. They occasionally overpaid, they withheld royalties for a while to recover, and Dad wrote letters asking them to explain what had just happened. Someone sent him a letter informing him about a class action suit against a group of oil companies for alleged fraud, and he and Rich had to talk about it. His royalty checks got lost, and he had to track them down. Mineral rights ownership in North Dakota is now so fractured—several generations of descendants have inherited the original rights—there must be occasions when nobody, not even the oil companies, can figure out who owns what or who lives where.

My dad wrote about a new horizontal drilling technique in 1990, his first mention of the coming revolution in domestic oil and gas production.

North Dakota has decided to adopt Texas' newest oil drilling technique, he wrote. *Down and then slant off sideways. Here's hoping.*

Dad didn't use the term "horizontal drilling," but he knew about the technique and was keeping his fingers crossed that it might successfully coax more oil from those stingy North Dakota rocks.

Eight months after he yearned in a backhanded way for higher oil revenue, he expressed a different sentiment:

The Middle East thing is about one thing and one thing only. Oil prices. If we, and the rest of the western world, had seriously started to be more efficient and had invested in alternative energy sources long ago, we wouldn't be worried about high oil prices ruining our economy.

At the time he expressed these contradictory thoughts, my father was not yet seventy and in full possession of his mental faculties.

And then there was my uncle Steve, born a dozen years after his Eagle Scout brothers. He managed neither his mineral rights nor his life very well. He could sing like an angel, but that talent was never enough to carry him past his troubles. For years, Dad and Rich had sent money to their mother to help support her, but they began to realize that the money always found its way to Steve, who squandered it. On what, I'm not sure. Cars and car repairs, fancy living, cigarettes.

Mother kept feeding him money, Uncle Rich says.

Did she know she was being taken advantage of? I ask.

Yes, Rich says. *She knew.*

What about her mineral rights? What did she do with those? I ask.

If Mother had any oil rights left, she had given them all to Steve, he says.

After my grandmother died, if Steve hadn't already hit bottom, he was now exploring the full dimensions of that miserable condition many of us glimpse at one time or another. He died in California of apparent heart failure. My uncle Steve was fifty-eight, divorced, obese, and also penniless.

When I try to remember how old Dad was when I lost him—that is, lost the closeness I had always felt with him—I can't quite pin it down.

Throughout the 1980s and 1990s, whenever I visited my parents, Dad would invite me into his darkroom so he could show me what kind of photographic mischief he had been up to. My father's darkroom was his man cave. Oscar had his ramshackle homesteader's shack on Westberg Farms; Dad had his darkroom.

I loved following Dad into this tiny space jammed with the implements of photography and black-and-white film developing—boxes of powdered chemicals, trays for mixing the chemicals, shelves for his old cameras and camera parts, and boxes, drawers, and files bulging with photographic paper, prints, and negatives. The focal point of the room was his two creaky enlargers, which he had clamped to a pockmarked table. He had pieced them together with duct tape from parts he'd scrounged decades earlier.

I also loved the familiar smell of the chemicals and the way the room could cut off the sights and sounds of the outside world. He showed me what he had been working on, but he didn't ever say much about his artistic decisions—he was never a teacher—so I had to ask questions if I wanted to learn anything.

Why did you make the roof pop on this one?

How did you make the roof pop?

Where did you shoot this one?

Why did you include the front of that truck in this one? Why didn't you just crop it here?

When I was in high school, Dad showed me his methodical film developing process. He closed the door tightly and tucked a towel under it, or even duct taped it, to ensure that no light seeped in when he was handling unprocessed film. He had already set the things he needed nearby so he wouldn't have to fumble in the dark. When he was ready, he flipped the switch, and we stood side by side in total darkness. I'm sure my pupils grew large as my eyes searched for meaning, but also out of childlike awe and fear. This was a foreign world, Dad's world. He wasn't exactly teaching me how to do this process, but he was letting me in on his secret world.

I always breathed a sigh of relief when the negatives were processed enough to turn on the amber safety light. Ah, here's the secret world again. Here are the trays, the enlargers, the cardboard boxes, and the files. I can see them in this new ghostly light.

I took a photography course in college and learned the whole film developing process again from people who were paid to teach me. But I can hardly summon up memories of

My father photographed the relics of industry like these oft-repaired grain elevators along the Mississippi River in St. Paul, Minnesota.
Walter Westberg

One of my father's favorite photographic subjects: a stack of pipes.
Walter Westberg

those classes. The sessions with my dad remain burned into me like a photographic image on film.

I lost Dad sometime after he and Mom moved to Florida in the mid-1980s, sometime after he started to lose his hearing and after his memory started to go. I don't blame the move to Florida, although I suppose physical distance must have played a role. It was more the way he aged. He couldn't hear well, so he grew more isolated and participated less in conversations. He couldn't remember much, so he didn't even want to start up the kinds of conversations that demanded recall of names and dates.

The long conversations Dad and I used to have about new scientific discoveries and the latest political craziness in Washington, the intimate talks we used to have while rid-

ing together in a car or walking on the beach at the river—we didn't have those anymore. Or we just had frustrating snippets of them.

As Dad got more and more frail, he didn't give up photography. He kept one camera and continued to shoot in color, and he edited his photos on the computer. But when he dismantled his darkroom, sold his equipment and his large-format cameras, when he gave up that secret world, my old dad no longer existed. I missed him.

When Dad was well into his eighties, the things he worried about changed.

He didn't go out shooting photos as often. I always asked if he'd been out, and more and more often the answer was no. He wasn't sure he could find his way back home. It was hard for him to tell me this. My dad was getting old, really old.

But you wouldn't have to drive anywhere to take photos, would you? I asked him. *Could you just look for shots close to home?*

He said yes, but it was a yes accompanied by a shrug. It wasn't the same.

I visited my parents in the winter—I'm not stupid. Central Florida is about fifty degrees warmer than Minnesota in January. After years of our encouraging them to move back to Minnesota to be closer to family, or at the very least to a place in Gainesville where they could get more help, they finally moved to a retirement apartment complex nearby where they no longer needed to cook for themselves or arrange for yard help. Dad worried they wouldn't be able to afford it.

My sister applied her considerable spreadsheet skills to that question. She calculated best- and worst-case scenarios, scenarios in which his oil income remained at its current levels

My sunbathing parents shortly after their move from Minnesota to Florida, 1986. Family photo

(and this was before the fracking frenzy), scenarios in which they'd have to sell their mineral rights in order to pay the rent. That was worst case.

In his last year of life, Dad worried about his memory but not oil. In 1999, he got his first horizontal wells, but they weren't drilled into the Bakken Shale. Several years later, he started receiving royalties on his first fracked Bakken well, the gold standard of North Dakota oil. Everybody seemed to be drilling new wells. With the combined techniques of horizontal drilling and hydraulic fracturing and continual improvements on the process, those tight North Dakota rocks yielded more oil than ever. He no longer had to send letter after letter to North Dakota oil developers urging them to drill a well or rework a well. Oil production in North Dakota shot up in 2009; Dad's oil income spiked a few years later.

When I visited, we sat on their back porch, vodka tonics nestled in our hands, egrets delicately picking their way across a nearby pond, and we talked about the new oil landscape in North Dakota.

Thank you, Oscar! Mom said over and over in a grateful reference to my grandfather, who was either forced or was naturally inclined to reinvent himself many times—from one-room schoolhouse teacher to homesteader to elected county official to car salesman to insurance salesman to hospital bill collector to wheeler-dealer farmer. Mom hoisted her glass, and we all toasted Oscar in his last version of himself: mineral rights owner.

Because Oscar finally got in on something, and because my father held on to the lion's share of his mineral rights for six decades, my parents no longer had to worry about spending their savings to pay the rent. We could change the alert status on my sister's spreadsheets from red to orange, maybe even yellow. Dad toddled off to the mailbox every day looking for oil checks, which had long amounted to tens and hundreds of dollars and now amounted to thousands and more thousands.

The mailbox also held letters from those long-silent oil brokers, who now offered to buy my father's mineral rights. Dad mentioned these offers in his letters to us. His memory had faded, but his hard-wired North Dakota oil logic hadn't. He understood that if people were suddenly offering to buy his mineral rights, demand for them must be going up, and therefore there was even more reason to hang onto them. Uncle Rich felt the same way.

On Dad's ninetieth birthday, some of us flew down to help him celebrate. We told him he could eat whatever he wanted for dinner.

Come on, Dad! Anything you want!

He chose McDonald's. We loaded up the buck-fifty burgers and fries in his old Styrofoam cooler, which he always brought along to keep the food warm. He bolted down his burger almost before anyone else in the room had even unwrapped theirs.

But as the spring and summer wore on, he ate less and less and started losing weight. Mom said he slept a lot, and he was often napping when I called down there. By fall of his ninetieth year, the suspected diagnosis of pancreatic cancer was confirmed. He considered treatment and surgery, and I shuddered at this discussion. He was so frail and so old. As much as I loved my father, I crossed my fingers that he wouldn't opt for the trauma of treatment, and eventually Mom and Dad decided to skip it. I wanted him, of course, to live out the rest of his days in relative comfort, but none of us had any experience with the disease, and we did not know how much time he had.

Uncertain times like this tend to prompt serious navel gazing, always at two in the morning.

When you consider the twelve hundred miles that separated these midwestern winter refugees from their children and grandchildren; when you imagine the seven states—Wisconsin, Illinois, Indiana, Kentucky, Tennessee, Georgia, and Florida—that my newly retired parents crossed in a station-wagon twenty-two years earlier; when one of them gets very sick and starts losing weight; when the stress of that illness starts to jab at their daily routine until the routine limps, stumbles, and falls; when you realize that, sure, they have friends down there, but their friends are almost as feeble as, or even more feeble than, they are, and those kind but ancient friends can't drive over in the middle of the night to take someone to the hospital—geez, they should be taken to the hospital themselves!—or make the zillions of phone calls that need to be made; when you know with dead certainty that long-distance conversations reveal some but not all of the truth about what's going on, that's when you start to wonder if the freedom and choices offered by a sprawling continent, relative affluence, and cheap energy can turn around and bite you. It's damn near un-American to say it.

I don't know—I truly don't know—if my dad worried about the pain of dying. I was too far away, I had already lost my dad, and my mother, elderly herself and now thrust into the role of primary caregiver, was already spinning around with her own stress.

In his early years in Florida, Dad complained often of anxiety, and he and I talked about relaxation techniques—yoga, breathing, mind tricks—but he hadn't talked about anxiety in recent years. Mostly he just told jokes. His memory for jokes was astonishing.

Whether he worried about pain, I don't know, but he never did experience the excruciating pain associated with this disease. The hospice doctor said that with pancreatic cancer, the tumor typically presses on a nerve, but with Dad, it must have been growing in a different direction. A significant blessing.

Of all the things Dad worried about in his final hours, he wasn't worried about whether he was loved. I was sure of this fact, and that knowledge keeps me from coming unhinged.

INDEMNITY CLAUSE

> The mineral developer agrees to protect the mineral owner from any and all lawful claims against the mineral developer for loss, injury or damage resulting from the activities of the mineral developer under this lease.

> *The oil company agrees to protect the mineral owner from any claims of damage resulting from its activities on the leased land.*

MCKENZIE COUNTY, NORTH DAKOTA

A drilling rig about a mile north of the highway towers over the wheat fields. Everything is horizontal in western North Dakota except drilling rigs, cell phone towers, and the massive thunderheads that swagger across the sky like outsized outlaws.

A native North Dakotan (I'll call her Betty) has invited me to join her family on a tour of this drilling operation just south of the Missouri River. Her family once farmed here and has retained mineral rights. She says a geologist is giving the tour. A geologist! Maybe he will offer a little geology lesson.

Dad never got such a tour on one of his own wells, and it's a shame. I'm convinced that half the reason he loved North Dakota oil was that he was such an engineering nerd.

I arrive early to get my bearings. I turn off a gravel road into a gravel driveway—no shortage of gravel in this state—and inch toward the drill site, which bristles with trailers and noisy machinery and bright lights even though it's the middle of the day. It looks like a temporary town. If civilization in this part of the country used to be organized around main streets, wheat farms, and churches, today it's organized around 140-foot drilling derricks. If the drilling operation strikes oil—and these days it typically does—the drill rig gives way to a pump, a natural gas flare, and an impressive flow of oil and money.

Right now, though, the salient point for me is not oil or money. It's trucks. As I approach the drill site, a semi parked near the rig rumbles to life. There's only one way out for the driver, and it's the driveway I'm on. I do a hasty five-point turn: forward, reverse, forward, reverse, forward, and out of there.

Because I'm leaving in such a hurry, there's no way for me to determine if this is the right drill site, so I decide that it must be. I'll come back in an hour and a half.

When I return, I enter the driveway again, not at all sure that it's smart, legal, or safe to do so. There's a nasty color-coded sign warning visitors about poisonous gases. It's set on

the yellow level (*poison gas may be encountered*). I can barely force myself to drive forward. I absolutely expect something to blow up.

The rig throbs with working machinery and looms over everything. Up on the platform, workers in hard hats guide a new section of drill pipe into the wellbore. It looks so dangerous, I can hardly make myself look at it. I get out and ask the nearest worker where the geologist (I'll call him Tom) is, and he directs me to the right trailer.

Betty and her family are already here, and Tom welcomes me. Just seeing normal people gathered in a normal way reassures me that I might live through this experience. Betty called the geologist ahead of time, told him I was a writer working on a book, and asked whether I could accompany the group. He generously agreed.

The trailer is cramped—all trailers probably are—but there's enough room for four computer monitors, which are lit up with drilling data as it streams in. A poster on the wall shows the layers of rock that the drill bit has already eaten through, the Lodgepole, the False Bakken. Tom's job is to tell the drillers where to drill, and on this site and most other western North Dakota drill sites today, the destination is the Middle Bakken.

Oil drillers point their drills down for about two miles. Then they make a long slow curve—the kickoff point—and drill horizontally for another two miles through the oil-bearing formation. Their goal is to keep the drill headed straight and true through the Middle Bakken layer—here it's only twenty-eight feet thick—but as we can see on Tom's screens, the drill wanders up and down quite a bit.

I've never given it a moment's thought before, but it must

Oil worker on an active drilling rig awaits a new section of drill pipe, McKenzie County, North Dakota. Lisa Westberg Peters be hell to keep a drill going in a desired direction when it's two miles beneath the surface of the earth. You can't exactly see it. This is the kind of engineering prowess that would have made Dad whistle.

Tom says they look for geologic and chemical clues that identify the Middle Bakken, things like the correct gamma signature. I write down those words—"gamma signature"—but I don't know what he's talking about. Later I discover that all rocks emit gamma rays, information that makes me question the wisdom of keeping a substantial rock collection in my living room. The Upper Bakken, an organic-rich black shale, typically emits more gamma rays than most rocks. The lighter-colored center of this sedimentary Oreo cookie, the dolomite layer of the Middle Bakken, has fewer radioactive elements and therefore a lower gamma ray signature. Once they find those clues, the drillers try to stay in the zone, as Tom puts it.

And every thirty feet, he pulls a sample from the drill cuttings to hand over to the state of North Dakota. The little brown envelopes of powdered rock fill a box in the back of the trailer.

I realize very quickly that I probably won't be able to ask the million or so questions I have. After all, this tour is for the family, the triumphant mineral rights owners, and I'm just tagging along. But it's hard not to ask questions about an operation that's so foreign and fascinating.

I finally do ask him a straight-up geology question when it seems relevant. *How deep was the ocean here when the Bakken Shale was laid down?*

There was no sea here, he says.

Say what? His response makes no sense to me.

The average automobile driver might not know—or care—how oil forms as long as her car has enough gasoline to get her to work in the morning, but a few words about the Bakken Shale might be in order:

Consultant points out horizontal drilling progress to visitors. The microscope is for examining cuttings brought up from underground rock formations. Lisa Westberg Peters

It's true, the shale didn't form in a deep blue sea. The sea may have been shallow, but it was absolutely a sea. When I think shallow, though, I think wading pool. So it might be more helpful to describe the sea in terms of the continent. When the Bakken sediments were forming—about 360 million years ago—much of the North American continent was flooded by the sea.

The future North Dakota was nowhere near its present position at the 45th parallel. It basked in the tropics near the equator and lay at the western edge of the future North America.

The Williston Basin was at the time a recess, a big bay, along this ancient coast. And in this bay, algae and other organisms lived out their lives, died, and then rained down on the seafloor for eons. In a quirk of geologic fate that benefits anyone who drives a car, this particular burial ground lacked oxygen, a great environment for preserving organic carbon.

The carbon-rich sediments subsided, forming a bowl shape. Other layers of sediment buried the Bakken layers, but it was another couple hundred million years before the layers got deep enough and warm enough in the hydrocarbon kitchen for serious oil and gas formation.

Today the federal government estimates that the Bakken holds three and a half billion barrels of oil beneath two states, North Dakota and Montana, and two Canadian provinces, Saskatchewan and Manitoba. The government estimates an even higher quantity of oil in the formation just below the Bakken.

Tom hands Betty and her family a sample of pulverized shale with its rich quantities of oil. The sample came from a depth of 10,900 feet. He calls it the source rock, the source of all the oil. The family beams. Oil equals money.

It's fossil fuel! Tom declares. *The dinosaurs died and gave us all that oil.*

Once again, I probably look a little dumbfounded. Oil does not come from dinosaur fossil bones, and besides, the earliest dinosaurs evolved at least a hundred million years after these layers of mud started piling up at the bottom of the sea.

Clearly it isn't this consultant's job to know earth history or to know what this spot on the planet looked like hundreds of millions of years ago. It's his job to interpret the data streaming into his monitors and, based on that data, to tell the drillers where to drill. I assume he is doing that part very well. The drilling is on schedule; everything seems to be going as planned. He has found the Middle Bakken—no small feat considering how thin it is—and after the well is completed, or fracked, a pump will soon be pulling cooked and pressed marine algae out of it.

Still, I'm a little surprised that someone with so much responsibility on a multimillion-dollar oil-drilling site could hold such strange ideas about earth history. But I probably shouldn't be. The North Dakota oil field is growing so fast, companies have had to hire people with no previous oil industry experience. Minnesota canoe guides take a break from guiding and come here to make some serious money as roughnecks. Wisconsin farmers and Montana waitresses leave their families behind to drive big trucks and make enough money to pay off mortgages and car debts.

Tom runs out to do some actual work, and another member of the drilling crew (I'll call him Bill) comes in to talk to the family.

He's a big, sturdy guy who looks to be in his mid-thirties. He stands in a corner of the trailer and tells the family he works for Halliburton. As I absorb that information, I start to feel as though I'm no longer among my people. Am I in the state where my great-grandfather opened a hardware store, where my grandfather homesteaded, where my dad and uncle jumped off garage roofs?

I'm in the state of oil. It may not be Big Oil—most of the companies responsible for this latest boom are the smaller ones—but it's definitely oil. And Halliburton fracks many, if not most, of the oil wells in North Dakota. This is Halliburton of Halliburton Loophole fame. Congress, at the request of former Halliburton CEO Vice President Dick Cheney, exempted hydraulic fracturing from the terms of the Safe Drinking Water Act. This is Halliburton, the company with its hands in everything, according to Bill himself.

Bill tells us he first worked for Halliburton on the North Slope of Alaska. My pen instantly stops taking oil-drilling notes and starts recording this question: *Is he the owner of the red Corvette with Alaska plates that zipped through Williston on Highway 2 a few days ago?* But I can't ask that question out loud.

Bill is the mud engineer on this drill site. Later I learn that mud is the casual term for drilling fluids. Tom had referred several times to the *nasty* fluids they use as they drill, nasty fluids that, in this case, include diesel fuel. Bill presumably is in charge of choosing the components of the mud and adjusting them as conditions change. And today it's also his job to chat up the customers.

How long before we see the royalties? one of them asks. An obvious question.

Bill demurs. First they have to finish drilling, which they expect to do by the end of the week, then they have to fracture the well, so it might be a couple of months. I'd say a little longer. My mother doesn't get royalty checks for at least six months after a well starts producing. I think the family will need to be patient.

Tom leads us back outside and, as our tour concludes, tells the family he's not a real geologist, that he's not trained in geology. The family doesn't care. They're focused on the fact that the drilling finishes this weekend, the fracking's next, and the money comes after that, but I'm relieved to hear it. My faith in academic geology departments has been restored.

The elder sisters, broad grins on their faces, pose with the drill rig in the background. I snap a few photos, Betty puts some of her oil-rich Bakken Shale sample into a baggie for me, and we say goodbye.

I wonder what questions my father would have asked today if this had been one of his wells. As a chemical engineer, he might have asked about the components of the drilling mud. But more likely he would have offered these gentlemen several unsolicited suggestions for cheaper ways to drill this well.

Both Dad and Uncle Rich would have killed to be here today. Rich is such an engineering geek, he even got a kick out of riding a tour boat through the U.S. Army Corps of Engineers lock at St. Anthony Falls on the Mississippi River in Minneapolis. That was a few years ago. My dad couldn't join us—too old, too frail.

I'm more inclined to kill to hear great music or eat barbecued spareribs the way my brother-in-law fixes them. But today I was standing in for my elders. And today, by the way, was indeed a day spent among my people. My people have been drilling oil in western North Dakota for sixty years. I just wasn't paying attention.

MAKOTI, NORTH DAKOTA

Once the oil drillers drill two miles down, two miles across, they start looking for proppants to frack their wells. Proppants don't really prop open the tiny fractures in the shale; it's more accurate to say they keep the fractures open. The most commonly used proppant is sand.

I visit Makoti, North Dakota, population 154. This small and remote town is the site of two new oil-related activities: an oil refinery being built west of town by the Three Affiliated Tribes of Mandan, Hidatsa, and Arikara Nation, and a U.S. Silica unloading site for frac sand.

I'd still like to bag up a handful of frac sand. I'm a sand collector, right? Years ago, when Americans started hearing that the hydraulic fracturing process typically involved high-pressure injections of water, chemicals, and sand, many people asked, *Water? How much? Chemicals? Which ones?* I asked, *Sand? What kind of sand?*

In case you thought all sand was the same, I'm here to tell you it's not.

My sample of Mississippi River sand is a jumble of minerals and grain sizes and includes tiny metal balls from sandblasting operations on the bridges overhead. My white-sugar sand from Florida is just bleached, busted-up shells. My black sand from Hawaii formed when hot lava spilled into the sea and shattered into a zillion angular fragments. If oil drillers were to inject this angry Polynesian goddess sand—all elbows—into their tiny fractures, it would prop open the fractures, no problem, but the oil and the money would not flow.

Frac sand from Minnesota and Wisconsin is beautiful sand

composed of pale—fawn-colored to cream—quartz grains with rough edges smoothed and rounded by yawning time, millions of years of swishing back and forth on ancient beaches. It's odd, but the macho American petrochemical industry uses the Mellow Elder of Sand to frack its wells.

This pure silica sand, unfortunately, has a sinister side. Silica dust is a potential health threat to anyone exposed to it for a period of time. The federal government has issued alerts to workers involved in the frac sand mining and hydraulic fracturing process.

Makoti is a very quiet place compared to my Minneapolis neighborhood. Because I live in a noisy place, Makoti doesn't feel real to me. People live here? This town is a destination for frac sand shipments? Why?

I stop in at the one bar in Makoti, which is open late morning. *Do they unload frac sand here?* I ask the bartender, not a question you usually pose to bartenders.

Yeah, he says, *but I don't know anything about it.* He cocks his head in the direction of the grain elevator across the railroad tracks and tells me to talk to the guy over there.

I walk into the grain elevator office, and sure enough, the man working there knows about the frac sand shipments. He even shows me where sand has spilled onto the tracks. *The upcoming harvest will interrupt sand deliveries,* he says. He will need these tracks for shipping North Dakota grain.

I scoop up a handful of frac sand shipped several hundred miles from Wisconsin to this remote spot in North Dakota, and I stash it in my backpack for its eventual trip back to Minneapolis. The sand I don't bag up, the sand sitting inside the railcars parked near the grain elevator, will be injected into oil wells to keep open escape routes for petroleum crude. New wells are drilled here at a furious pace because fracked wells in North Dakota apparently produce like gangbusters for less than a year, and then production drops off. Time to poke a new hole in the earth, or time to rework the old wells. It's a very expensive process.

———————

WILLISTON, NORTH DAKOTA
There can't be many towns in the United States where you can go to a coffee shop and chat with a hydraulic fracturing expert over an iced coffee. Williston is one of them.

I have arranged to meet with Monte Besler, who helps oil companies frack their wells, mostly in the Bakken Formation. It's the hydraulic fracturing that triggers both oil production and the start of royalties to mineral owners all over the oil patch. Fracking triggers the wealth. My writing project is personal, but Monte knows that I have a strong interest in geology and want to hear about his job and North Dakota-style fracking.

I am nervous to meet him. Petroleum engineers and environmentally inclined writers speak a different language. Engineers speak in physics; I speak in subjects, verbs, and, if things get tricky, a dependent clause or two. Petroleum engineers spend day and night calculating the best way to get the most oil out of the ground; I would rather watch birds.

But, I told myself, if the gap between Monte and me proved too large, there was always sand. He's a fracking consultant; he must love sand, too.

He has the day off, so he walks into the Meg-A-Latte wearing casual clothes—shorts, a baseball cap that says "U.S. Border Patrol," and a T-shirt with a big eagle and the word "America" splashed all over it.

And we're off.

Monte tells me he grew up on a South Dakota ranch and graduated from the South Dakota School of Mines and Technology in the 1970s. He has stuck with the Great Plains oil industry through its booms and busts. He worked for several companies, including Halliburton, but a few years after the fracking-induced drilling surge began, he started his own consulting company, FRACN8R.

Monte says he completes three or four wells a month. *That's about all I can do,* he says. The work, not surprisingly, sounds lucrative. *I make more money in one day than I made in one month when I started out,* he says.

I ask him to try to describe the North Dakota hydraulic fracturing process, but whenever anyone orders a cappuccino or a latte, the espresso machine hisses out half his descriptions of steel casing, sleeve packers, horizontal stresses, vertical stresses, tectonic strain maps, and flowback water.

Monte starts talking about the horizontal and vertical pressures underground. Drilling deep into the earth requires an understanding of the competing pressures. He calls it *squish versus squash.* They even have to factor in plate tectonics when they drill a well.

The whole continent is moving northeast to southwest. Ideally you'd want to drill perpendicular to the direction of the continent movement, but you can't do that because of the way townships are formed, he says.

It's true. When Thomas Jefferson dreamed up our public land survey system, he didn't exactly factor in the slow movement of the continent.

I understand the general idea of plate tectonics. In fact, my fascination with the beauty and power of geology began when I did a ninth grade science project on continental drift. Who knew that the continents once fit together like puzzle pieces, drifted apart, and continue to drift? To factor in the stresses of continental movement in one of the most tectonically stable states in the country, is that trying too hard?

As much as I want to understand everything, I don't. But if I could take a layperson's stab at what Monte said about the fracturing process, it would go something like this:

After they drill the well, they send down charges—explosives—at specific intervals. They set off the explosives, which, at six million pounds of pressure per square inch at the tips of the charges, are easily strong enough to punch holes in the well's steel casing.

The explosions create two- to three-foot-long finger-sized holes—Monte refers to them as *tunnels*—which extend into the surrounding rock. But that's not the end of the fracturing.

Next comes the slurry of water, sand, and chemicals, the stew of stuff that's generated so much controversy across the country. The slurry is injected with great force into the well. The water is the delivery system for the chemicals and the sand. The pressure forces the slurry into the short tunnels and increases their length to two to three hundred feet from the casing. Most of the sand stays in the cracks, keeping them open against the intense pressure of the earth, which would otherwise close the fractures. Once the tight rock is fractured, the oil in the rock finds escape routes, and well operators pump it out.

I tell Monte that I've seen red trucks bristling with tubes and instruments in the oil-field traffic stream in Williston. *When they frack a well, do they use those odd-looking trucks?* I ask.

Monte says I'm describing the downhole blender. *They're pricey pieces of equipment, well in excess of a half million each, probably approaching one million. They're the heart of the fracking job. The truck's equipment mixes and pumps the chemicals, proppant, and water into the well at high pressure. If you saw the red trucks, those were Halliburton. Another company uses red and green trucks. They're the butt-ugliest trucks. They don't even look good at Christmas.*

For this coffee shop conversation, we don't have time to cover all things fracking, so I don't dwell on questions about the chemicals, the high volumes of water, and the potential for groundwater pollution. We aren't going to agree on most of those issues, but I do want to ask about the sand. Monte's a fracking consultant; he must like sand.

I'm wrong. Monte says he doesn't like sand for fracking in North Dakota. Here I am, in the middle of a state lousy with petroleum engineers, and I find one who doesn't like sand.

To remind you, I have serious qualms about our country's renewed infatuation with fossil fuel, but in this weird ambivalence I have felt since the start of my trip, I find I'm disappointed. What about Minnesota and Wisconsin sand? We have the best frac sand in the world!

He explains. In North Dakota, the depths are so great and the pressures so enormous, the sand crushes. He's seen crushed silica sand in North Dakota oil wells that causes pumping equipment to fail and require replacement, in some cases many times. Man-made proppants will also crush, he says, but to a much lesser degree and into larger pieces that are less troublesome to pumping equipment.

I don't know whether Monte's right about the sand, but I'm quite sure that if you're in a rush to drill, produce oil, and make money, the cheaper proppant is going to be the tempting choice.

One oil producer in the Bakken so firmly believes in sand for fracking wells in North Dakota, it also owns sand mines in Minnesota and Wisconsin. And of course U.S. Silica, a profitable U.S. corporation, is hauling railcars full of the stuff from Wisconsin to the Bakken oil field.

Monte says he prefers man-made materials—ceramic proppants—and more specifically, proppants made by domestic manufacturers. The quality control of the Chinese manufacturers, he says, is a little sketchy. *I've found bolts in it, gravel in it, rubber Super Balls in it.*

I have already seen bags of the Chinese proppant stacked up at Williston's railroad depot, waiting for delivery to new drilling sites.

We've been talking for an hour and a half, and that godawful steam machine has been hissing for at least half the time. I'm not a reporter. It's not my job to pin this fracking expert down, so I ask him why he likes his job.

Bags of ceramic proppant for the hydraulic fracturing process, stacked near the Williston train depot. Lisa Westberg Peters

I like it because it's not manufacturing, he says. *It's engineering. There's what we know, what we think we know, and what we don't know. I like using my engineering training and my experience and my intuition to overcome the uncertainty.*

Monte doesn't like that people think of oil industry workers as knuckle-dragging Neanderthals. He talks about how he checks fifteen to twenty computer screens in the van during a frack job.

Wouldn't you like to actually see those rocks ten thousand feet down? I ask.

Yeah, I'd love to, he says.

Monte seems very confident that fracturing isn't contaminating groundwater in North Dakota. *If you have a contamination incident, it's with the old wells, the abandoned ones,* he says.

I start to wonder whether any of Oscar's old abandoned wells on the Nesson Anticline are leaking something into the groundwater. What would anybody do to fix the damage? And what would be our liability in that situation? Nobody would sue us, right? Isn't that what the indemnity clause is for? I'd better take another look at that ancient oil lease. Had they come up with the indemnity clause by 1950?

We stray into the subject of climate change, and of course, we don't agree. Monte thinks the climate has been warming since the end of the ice ages and that we humans give ourselves too much credit for being able to change it. *We're not as important as we think we are.* And I think that the rapid climate changes we see today are directly related to our habit of burning fossil fuel. We can measure the changes with our fancy instruments, but the problem is so big—the environmental elephant in the room—we're having trouble grasping it. And what's our liability to future generations if we don't get this right?

As usual, I have more questions than answers. Perhaps because I'm exhausted, I ramble on about my family's oil interests and my grandfather's farm, and I mention that my mother has started getting checks for a new well.

He perks up. *What's the name of the well?*

When I tell him the name, he says, *I fracked that well.*

Wouldn't you know? I find a petroleum engineer who doesn't like sand, but he did frack my mom's latest well. North Dakota is a 71,000-square-mile small town. They say there are only two degrees of separation between North Dakotans, not the usual six. And I've already started to recognize a dozen longtime North Dakota names in newspaper articles, maps, and census forms from my grandfather's day, their descendants bouncing around today. Descendants like me.

Nonetheless, I'm so surprised, I almost forget to ask, *How did it go? My mother's well?*

Good, Monte says. *It was December, cold weather at the time.*

We were down well below zero. It's a twenty-four-hour operation, but on this one, I went home at night. A lot of other supervision does stay out there.

He started at six one evening and finished six days later in the middle of the night. He fracked the well in thirty stages using two different techniques. Multistage fracking is expensive and time consuming, but North Dakota drillers have learned that it increases production. And he used several sizes of both ceramic proppant and Wisconsin sand. *Sand is still not my favorite choice, but it's far more durable there than other areas.* The well is shallower than others in the Williston Basin, which means lower pressures and temperatures.

Later, Monte sends me the information submitted by the oil company to North Dakota regulators in Bismarck. For this fracturing job, the drillers used almost three million pounds of proppant, both sand and man-made ceramics. Monte said that amounted to about sixty-three truck trips. The well's operator voluntarily reported to the website FracFocus that the hydraulic fracturing required almost three million gallons of water and about thirty chemicals.

In its first month, this well produced about seven hundred barrels of oil per day.

I have been reading news articles and checking websites on the technique of hydraulic fracturing for years, and I've grown numb to the numbers. There's the total amount of water and chemicals and proppants, and then there's the concentration of chemicals and proppants in the fracturing fluid. The decimals are carried out to the nth place. An ingredient concentration is never listed at *about 60 percent*. It's 58.84186 percent.

My eyes tend to glaze over at all these numbers, but self-indulgent eye-glazing might not be appropriate anymore. The engineer who sat across from me on a coffee shop couch in Williston helped determine the numbers. And these are not just his numbers; they're my family's numbers. His oil activity is my oil activity.

Our sand trucks—sixty-three of them—rumbled past my grandfather's land, *our* proppants were injected into my mother's oil well, and *our* oil is now in tanker cars rolling across the plains and through the neighborhoods of my city.

We were suddenly speaking the same language.

SECONDARY TERM

> The mineral developer leases from the mineral owner for a primary term and as long thereafter as oil and/or gas may be produced in commercial quantities . . .

> *Discovery of minerals during the primary term triggers the secondary term, and royalties for the mineral owner. A lease stays alive as long as the mineral developer keeps producing minerals in commercial quantities.*

WILLIAMS COUNTY, NORTH DAKOTA

Time to grab hold of the ropes again.

My family—for now, just eleven of us in three cars—pulls out onto U.S. Highway 2 in Williston, and we all drive like hell, which is how everyone drives these days on Highway 2. Very quickly, the stream of trucks carrying frac sand, mobile homes, petroleum crude, and dismantled drilling rigs separates us.

Our only plan for this Great Plains funeral is to caravan south from Williston to Theodore Roosevelt National Park and sprinkle Dad's ashes. He had a slender connection to the place. In the 1930s, Dad and Rich traveled, probably in a caravan of Model Ts, with the Williston Junior Municipal Band to this northernmost display of badlands scenery to play at dedication ceremonies. Besides, it's a spectacular place.

That *was* our plan, but we're headed north.

Three of us—my sister-in-law and her two daughters—are on the Amtrak train, which is going to be late to Williston. The prospect of a bunch of antsy people waiting around for an extra hour in this dusty oil town feels like a bad idea, so my brother stays behind to wait for his family, and the rest of us move on. The new plan is to try to find Oscar's old farmstead and a family oil well or two near Tioga, about fifty miles northeast of Williston. When the train riders join us, we'll go to the national park.

Going anywhere with eleven people in three cars—even roped together by common purpose and cell phones—is never a point A to point B thing. Somebody's hungry, so we stop for lunch at the 42 Grill in Tioga, the town that giddily labeled itself the oil capital of North Dakota in the 1950s after oil was discovered a few miles south of there.

As we wait and wait and wait for lunch to arrive, we continue our new North Dakota game: counting and categorizing extended cab trucks, the *de rigueur* passenger vehicle here. Ford, Dodge, and GMC all lag behind the clear winner, Chevy. The service is so slow, my son-in-law has time to draw a generic extended cab truck and label the parts that distinguish one model from another. We probably have time to test-drive an extended cab truck.

I cross the street to get a closer look at a flatbed truck loaded with big wooden boxes labeled "FRAC STRING."

What's frac string? I ask the guys near the truck.

It's . . . it's . . .

Oil workers not accustomed to explaining things to civilians.

It's used for fracking? I say, trying to be friendly.

Yeah, yeah . . .

They nod, apparently warming to the idea of educating a passerby about their work.

I nod, too, and wait.

It's like pipe! one of them finally bursts out, coming up with a word that any idiot ought to know.

I smile and thank them. I *know* it's pipe, but now my brain is wondering if oil drillers don't call pipe "pipe." Do they call it "string"? I walk back to the restaurant because it's clear that it would take a while for them to explain to me how that pipe/string is actually used in the fracking process, more time than they have and maybe even more time than it will take for our waitress to bring our food.

Flatbed truck carrying drilling supplies parked on a street in Tioga, North Dakota. Lisa Westberg Peters

She finally does bring our burgers and grilled chicken sandwiches and fries. She's from Bismarck, here for the summer to make money. If I were her, I'd have quit already, not wanting to deal with dust and cranky customers. She smiles and hands out plates of food to us, wide-eyed oil patch tourists. She's also serving the people who are working in the area, guys in Halliburton outfits and other burly guys who just have to be oil patch workers. The place is jumping.

We're finally on our way again, our caravan heading north on State Route 40, and very quickly one of our ropes—the cell phone—starts to fray. I'm getting no reception. Not very many people live in North Dakota—less than a million statewide—and that translates to about ten people per square mile. What this means to me is that cell phone companies did a cost-benefit analysis for this spot and came up mostly cost, not much benefit.

In the weeks before we all started the journey to western North Dakota, I asked my sister and two brothers if they had any thoughts about how the ash-sprinkling day should go. How should we do it? But nobody had strong thoughts, and we're not a formal bunch. A spreadsheet couldn't help us now.

I was forced to ask the Internet, where one click leads to another, and I stumbled across a twelfth-century neo-Confucian scholar named Zhu Xi, who made his mark by writing down funeral instructions for the common folk. My open-ended search for funeral advice might have ended there, but I live near a university, and one of the advantages is not the streets clogged with skateboarding students, obviously, but the ease with which I can hop on a bicycle, ride a mile and a half, and find Zhu Xi's instructions in the stacks of a huge library.

Zhu Xi recommended that demon-quellers lead a funeral procession and that everybody ride in carriages or on horses. On the road, he advised, wail whenever grief is felt.

Today I am the leader of this caravan of cars because, out of this party of reasonably intelligent people, I'm the only one with a good map: the *North Dakota Atlas and Gazetteer*. As we head north, I cross-reference the map with my printouts of oil wells and Uncle Rich's hunches issued on a regular basis from the backseat, and we turn left off the state road onto a gravel road. But the road quickly degenerates into two dirt tracks, a farm road. Bright yellow canola fields surround us.

I stop and get out of the car. I wave my arms and my useless cell phone and shout to the caravaners behind us, *Just kidding!* Three cars have to back up onto State Route 40.

We try the next left. Two miles down this new gravel road, we see an oil well on the left with a name my sister recognizes. She says Dad knew this well and was getting royalties from it. It was drilled into the Bakken Shale in 2010, the operator

Oil worker at a horizontal Bakken well near Tioga that pays royalties to my mother. Lisa Westberg Peters

struck oil, the pumpjack started pumping, and the secondary term in Dad's lease kicked in.

An oil worker (I'll call him Carl) is on site, checking something—gauges, instruments, valves?—on the storage tanks, and I'm not sure whether it's good or bad that a worker is here. Will he (1) give us a tour or (2) boot us off the property? After all, our family never owned the surface rights here, and our mineral rights are on adjacent property, but because of the way the state of North Dakota regulates the industry, my mother now receives checks from the oil pumped from this horizontal well.

We pull in. Carl, who describes himself as a pumper, chooses Option 1—the tour—and abandons his gauge-checking duties.

This is what's in the storage tanks, here's where we separate the oil from the natural gas and the water, and so on. Uncle Rich is a kid in a candy shop. He stands close, partly because his hearing isn't good but also because he's a kid in a candy shop.

It's different for me.

First I take pictures, and then I take notes, then pictures, then notes, a multitasking seesaw that reflects my ambivalence.

Wow, he's got some actual North Dakota oil, our oil, in that plastic bottle. Very cool! I want to hold that bottle!

Wait, he's got some North Dakota oil, our oil, in that bottle, our own contribution to the fracking frenzy.

Wow, that oil is almost pretty. It's almost green, and it's fizzy with natural gas.

Pretty? How can petroleum crude be pretty?

In my photos, I get horizons tilted first one way, then the other. I take ragged, incomplete notes, and I have an unambivalent headache.

The afternoon and the tour wind on. We follow Carl over to the neighboring oil well, this one located on my grandfather's former property and also producing income for my mother. Carl calls it his baby. It's newer and produces about five hundred barrels of crude oil per day, more than the first well we saw. Natural gas from underground is being flared off because, so far, there isn't a pipeline to carry it to markets. The orange flare hisses. It's one of the hundreds of flares and active drilling rigs recently recorded by a NASA satellite. Western North Dakota shines like New York City.

I see a car and an accompanying cloud of dust on the gravel road heading toward us. My brother is finally delivering the Amtrak riders after their long train trip across the plains. They say they're not tired, and I think they're lying, but now I'm beginning to realize it's at least two hours from here to the national park, our chosen ash-sprinkling site, and that's only if we don't get lost or have to stop again to eat or pee, and what are the odds of that? Where did the afternoon go? I pull back from the oil well tour and wonder what the hell we should do about this funeral.

Zhu Xi disapproved of cremation, but he did offer advice on how to choose a proper burial site. Discover the excellence of the land, he said, and ensure that the spot is never made into a road, a wall, or a ditch, and that it's never cultivated.

After Carl drives off, perhaps to check on a new well, my sister and I huddle and then circulate among the group with a new plan. What if we sprinkle the ashes right here at the edge of the canola field? Except for the gas flare and the rhythm of the pumpjack, it's quiet. We had expected noise and traffic and general unpleasantness here in the heart of the oil patch, but that's not what we're finding today. I have seen only one oil-field truck go by. This spot has big sky beauty, and best of all, it's right here, not more than a hundred miles from here.

Nobody objects. New plan: sprinkle Dad's ashes next to one of his cherished oil wells.

Zhu Xi's instructions for graves were very specific. You were to dig a rectangular pit and line it with cement made from a mixture of lime, sand, and yellow earth so that neither ants nor robbers could enter.

Before we left Minneapolis, I visited a half dozen stores in the Twin Cities, searching for a suitable container for the ashes. The cardboard container didn't seem special enough for a ceremony. I found myself in a discount gift store staring at a shelf full of baskets. I call my sister.

Do you have a sec? I ask.

Yes, she says.

What if I describe a basket to you and you tell me whether it sounds good for a container for Dad's ashes?

OK, she says.

It's round, I say, *about a foot in diameter, six inches high, it's made of woven basket-type material, you know, whatever baskets are made of, and it has a lid. It's simple, not fancy, but it's nice, not tacky.*

My sister is the finest human being alive for knowing when it's clear beyond a reasonable doubt that words of support are in order.

That sounds good, she says. *It sounds just right.*

Encouraged, I go on.

It looks like something Mom would have picked up at the Waldo flea market saying, "Let's get this, Walt! It's perfect." She would have paid a buck fifty for it, filled it with rocks and shells from Florida beaches, and set it on their porch.

I can pretty much see my sister smile over the phone. And so I buy it.

Zhu Xi told his readers to take a new attitude toward burial goods. Scale back and simplify, he said. Avoid precious objects, for they would just be a burden to the dead. His followers buried their loved ones with the artifacts of everyday life, things like ceramic vessels, iron scissors, and bronze spoons.

My sister plucks a handful of sunflowers from a ditch alongside the gravel road. They are grave goods of convenience, to be sure, but she loves sunflowers. Wherever she lives, the same basket of silk sunflowers appears on her kitchen counter. Today these humble flowers from a ditch feel satisfying.

I lift the basket with cremated remains from the trunk of the car, an act I have never before performed.

I feel a part of myself step back from the part of me that's removing my father's ashes from the car.

I watch as that person, Lisa, lifts out the basket of ashes, and Dave stands beside her to help if she needs it.

And now she's walking slowly, carrying the basket, and it takes her forever to walk those few steps from her car and past her family to the edge of the canola field where oil and farming meet.

The members of her family begin to organize themselves into small clumps like planets, and they begin to orbit around the basket as though it's generating a gravitational pull, and her husband and her brother begin to cut open the bag of ashes, but the plastic is thick and hard to cut, and it's firmly fastened at the top with a metal fastener, and all she hears is the sound of the knife jabbing at the plastic, and all she sees is what's right in front of her eyes. She hands a small garden trowel to her uncle Rich, the eldest in this group, and he takes the first scoop of ashes.

It's been nice knowin' ya, Rich says in direct communication with his brother. Smiling, he flings the ashes into the air, up and over the field. Some of the heavier particles of ash fall quickly onto the field, but an arc of smaller, lighter particles lingers in the air, drifting a bit in the breeze. Then he tosses one of the sunflowers into the field.

The planets wobble, adjust, rotate.

My father's ashes drift over a canola field on a cloudless North Dakota day in July. Antonio Rodriguez

After her uncle, each of her family members tosses a sunflower along with a trowelful of ashes into the canola field. There are gloves for the squeamish. Everyone knows there are gloves, but no one asks for them.

With her left hand, Lisa tosses a trowelful of ashes. With her right hand, she tosses first a sunflower and then her own burial good, also brought here in the trunk of the car. The white mask, a descendant of her father's most enduring and most recognized invention, a soft white mound, lands in

Westberg clan at the site of our ash-sprinkling ceremony, north of Tioga, North Dakota. Anonymous photographer

a dark furrow of the field and sits, out of place, like one of those mushrooms that pops up instantaneously after a rain. This simple attempt at ritual—tossing a sunflower and a white mask—even this much ceremony would have made her unsentimental father squirm. Today she and her family have to depart from his unsentimental approach to life in order to acknowledge his talents.

I watch all this.

I see the planets orbiting, shifting, reorganizing, and I hear the pumpjack nodding up, then down, then up, then down, a rhythm it maintains throughout the year and every year, even if there are three feet of snow on the ground, even if the crops have dried up, even if an elderly farmer nearby happens to die and the funeral procession files past it.

My dad's equally steady rhythm sustained him through sixty years of marriage, fatherhood, and a long career. If the purpose of a eulogy is to praise the person who has recently died and if imitation is a form of praise, this mechanical icon of the oil industry delivers the eulogy today.

I hear my son-in-law click the shutter of his camera to record the arcing ashes against the sky and fields, and I see my sister-in-law place something on the ground, a button she received from Dad that says, *I am loved,* and I see the ashes of my grief-soaked haiku and the notebook paper it's written on—tucked into my father's pocket just after he died—rise into the air along with my father's.

And I hear an English horn, somewhere, nowhere, begin a plaintive melody that wanders across the afternoon. Another horn follows it, and the orchestra finally takes up the same path. I know this melody. I know it, but what is it? And my brain cells finally line up—it's Dvorak's ninth symphony, but it's called the *New World Symphony* because the composer wrote this music soon after arriving on American soil, around the time my Swedish immigrant clan was turning over the thick prairie sod on their western Minnesota homestead, around the time Oscar was a youngster, just eight, but probably already knowing he wanted to go west.

And I hear this description of the melody:

> Here were the sand hills, the grasshoppers and locusts, all the things that wakened and chirped in the early morning; the reaching and reaching of high plains, the immeasurable yearning of all flat lands. There was home in it, too; first memories, first mornings long ago; the amazement of a new soul in a new world . . . a soul obsessed by what it did not know, under the cloud of a past it could not recall.

Did you ever read Willa Cather, Dad? I ask.

And do you remember playing this melody? How could you ever forget? You fretted, sweated bullets, and you did just fine because you worked so hard to prepare for it. You loved this music, too.

But I'm the one who feels the yearning of these flat lands, and I'm the one who was searching for home when I began this journey across the Midwest, and I'm the one who wanted to find the missing threads of our family's first memories—lost by illiteracy, deliberate silence, and my own inattention—and I'm the one who finds a new world here.

I see how I got here, Dad, but I'm still not sure where I'm headed.

IN WITNESS WHEREOF

> In witness whereof, this instrument is executed as of the date first above written.
>
> *The traditional beginning of the concluding clause of a will or contract, especially a deed.*
>
> BLACK'S LAW DICTIONARY, TENTH EDITION

DRIVING EAST FROM WILLISTON, NORTH DAKOTA, TO MINNEAPOLIS

After our oil patch funeral, I stayed on for a few weeks, but my family left Williston by twos and threes, by car and train, and Uncle Rich was the last.

On the morning of his departure, we sat together in the grim little breakfast room of the motel. He was headed first to Grand Forks, where his wife, my aunt, is buried, and then back to Pennsylvania. He kept assuring me that he loved to drive. *I'm more comfortable driving than walking.* I wasn't exactly reassured. He was a ninety-year-old driving across the country alone.

We walked over to his car in the parking lot. I could see clean shirts hanging from a pole that stretched across his backseat, everything neat and in perfect order. Did he learn how to set up this traveling closet from his father? Oscar must have needed a clean shirt every day when he was working the customers as a traveling salesman.

We hugged goodbye. Then Rich pulled out of the parking lot and turned onto U.S. Highway 2. I watched him successfully navigate the traffic, and I stood in the parking lot, watching long after I could no longer see his car.

Several days later, Dave called me from Minneapolis to say that Rich had left a message and had indeed made it home.

Now it's my turn to go home. My research here is finished.

I don't have a backseat closet. I jam my clothes into a suitcase. How come clothes fit in the suitcase when you first pack them but not when you're repacking to go home? Does dirty underwear take more space than clean underwear?

BISMARCK, NORTH DAKOTA

I must be a red-blooded, frontier-loving American. Heading west wakes me up; heading east makes me tired. Because I'm such a wimp, this six-hundred-mile solo trip from western North Dakota back home to Minneapolis will take me two days.

When we were in our twenties, Dave and I pulled an all-nighter driving across North Dakota. It was July. By midnight the sky was *finally* dark, the northern lights started to shimmer purple and green, our radio started playing the "Russian Sailor's Dance," and that combination of unearthly glow and feverish music? Well, it was another one of those times we nearly went off the road on the Great Plains.

JAMESTOWN, NORTH DAKOTA

I don't stop for lunch. I just eat whatever I can dig out of my backpack—apples, cheese, crackers—and keep driving.

And I'm not in the mood for sparks. Instead of listening to B. B. King rock this world of wheat, I replay some of my conversations with North Dakotans.

Williams County farmer:

I'll admit that I do have minerals. It makes quite a little difference in their attitude toward the oil drilling if people own minerals or not. You can't blame them. If they don't have minerals, they're getting all the disadvantages, the traffic, and the noise. That's human nature.

Retired North Dakota oil and gas attorney:
We all think about climate change. We consume too much energy, but you can't store electricity. I would accelerate the changeover from automobiles, but at this point you have no substitute.

Bismarck writer:
You'd have to change human nature, so we don't want so much stuff. It would have to be a fundamental shift. That's usually a long-term thing. And first there has to be an adverse effect.

Seventy-eight-year-old Williston resident:
This oil boom, it's all about the money.

Williams County farmer who owns surface rights:
You can't do anything about it.

And one of the last conversations I had:
Did you know my grandfather, Oscar Westberg?
Yeah, says the elderly farmer who stands at the door of his house.

Finding someone in North Dakota who knew my grandfather turned out to be as simple as knocking on the door of the house across the road from Oscar's farm. Just when you're starting to think life is too hard to hit—ninety-mile-an-hour fastballs, and who can see 'em?—a fat one crosses the plate.

This man looks a little surprised to see me, a complete stranger, standing on his back steps. It probably doesn't happen that often, someone wandering in off the road like this.

Leon is slender with wispy gray hair and wears a red-checked shirt, jeans, and big, unfashionable glasses. Eventually, he relaxes enough to show me a slightly crooked smile. I take another minute to explain why I'm prowling around his countryside, book project, blah blah blah, and he accepts all that.

What was Oscar like? I ask, still a little incredulous.

He was a likable guy, Leon says. *Cheerful.*

Leon might be a man who doesn't toss around excess verbiage. But he goes on.

I was just a kid, he says, *but I remember when they bought the land. A father and son were living in the homesteader's shack, probably renters. When Oscar and his partner bought the land, the father and son moved out.*

Oscar and Stevie would come by and visit, he says. I completely forget my manners and ask Leon how old he is. He says seventy-seven, and I do the math. He and my uncle Steve would have been about the same age. Leon doesn't remember Dad and Rich. They were older and off to college. And Meg didn't come out as often.

He couldn't always keep up with the combining. Leon pauses. *Your grandfather was quite talkative.* I can see how loquaciousness might interfere with combining and also make an impression on a quiet, thoughtful kid, which Leon must have been.

Leon's wife, Larena, joins us on the back stoop. They invite me into the house, which strikes me as generous. It's midsummer; the crops are in, but I figure farmers always have a million things to do.

We pass through the kitchen, and Leon and I sit at a dining room table just off the main living space. It's comfortable in here because the room looks lived in, not the kind of room saved for company. It's also a little dark, small windows and all, and today that feels cozy.

Larena offers to make me a ham sandwich—maybe my growling stomach has betrayed my hunger—and then she disappears into her office. She's a CPA and has work to do.

Leon and I sit at the table. Our conversation ranges from the price of farmland to the mysteries of mineral rights. He tells me more about the 1957 lease for the 1955 well. The well sits about a mile south of Leon's farmhouse and is named after his grandmother. The well's operator decided the well was pulling oil from a larger subsurface area than originally thought, so it expanded the pool of mineral owners to include my family, whose land lay just east of the well. The well is still producing almost sixty years later and earning royalties for my family.

We shift to the present.

The oil boom, I say to Leon, *what do you think about it?*

He looks straight at me as he says, *We would have been better off without it.* When I posed this question to other western North Dakotans, they typically shrugged and said something like this: *It's OK . . . I wish it were going a little slower.*

If North Dakotans are earning royalties, they tend to like the oil boom and forgive its inconveniences; if they're not, they tend not to. But Leon is a mineral rights owner. He earns royalties when the oil drillers strike oil.

What do you mean? I ask him.

At first he talks about the disruption of their quiet lifestyle— the truck traffic, the wrecked roads, the increased crime, and the litter left by the oil workers near the well pads. I picture my own Minneapolis neighborhood and the empty plastic bottles tossed here and there by oblivious students or visitors. As my nephew once put it, *Didn't their moms teach them?*

Leon and Larena liked the quiet life, and for the most part, it's gone.

I don't blame the truckers, he says. *They're just doing their jobs.* And he says he appreciates that people who need jobs are finding them. Some of them have families. They're not all single males who might be more inclined to drink off the paycheck and make trouble.

But Leon repeats what he just said: *We would have been better off without it.* And this time he's looking beyond the litter and traffic.

You can see what's happening in the world, he says. *The climate has changed a lot in my lifetime. There are more weather extremes, and my opinion is backed up by the evidence.*

I haven't heard a card-carrying North Dakota mineral rights owner talk about the changing climate. It's almost a forbidden subject.

I don't think many North Dakotans would agree with you, I tell him. Or at the very least, I add, not very many would be willing to say it out loud, given how much money is pouring into their bank accounts. Those royalties are fueling vacations to Alaska and Hawaii, the purchase of new trucks, and college educations for children, grandchildren, nieces, and nephews.

People don't want to believe in climate change, he says. *It's nice that we're more energy independent.* This is as close as Leon gets to ambivalence. *But with the renewed fossil fuel activity, the alternative energy gets stifled.*

He hasn't heard that water supplies are being contaminated from hydraulic fracturing or the injection of salty and chemical-laden wastewater back into the earth. *It makes me uncomfortable,* he says, *but it hasn't happened yet.*

I haven't heard anything, either. The Bakken Shale and the aquifers in Williams County are separated by several thousand feet. If operators do their jobs properly, aquifers shouldn't become contaminated. But they don't always do their jobs properly.

And for the third time, in case I missed his opinion of North Dakota's latest, and by far largest, oil boom, Leon says, *We would have been better off without it.*

Leon and I sit together at his table. Larena is still working in the next room. I finish the sandwich, which I figure saved my life today, and push the plate aside. Whatever is happening outside—new wells being drilled, old ones being maintained, pumpjacks pumping—we can't hear it right now. It's very quiet in the room.

VALLEY CITY, NORTH DAKOTA

A sign on the eastbound side of the freeway interrupts my thoughts with the billboard equivalent of a cymbal crash. BE POLITE, it says in boxy black letters. Not sure who wasted his or her hard-earned money on this message because North Dakotans are polite to a fault. To be sure, regulators started regulating early on in the hunt for oil, but for the most part, the state's message to the oil and gas industry is, *You may tentatively tell us what you have in mind.* This overly solicitous Mother Hubbard attitude expressed in my grandfather's words seems so 1955.

Oscar didn't know that burning his beloved oil in his beloved touring cars would help stir up atmospheric mayhem. Fifty years later, my father understood CO_2's truly annoying trick of trapping heat, but the hard years of the Depression and Dust Bowl left scars. Those scars allowed him to avert his eyes.

Today my eyes are wide open as I travel this straight-as-a-fence road.

FARGO-MOORHEAD

Back in Minnesota . . . am I out of the range of the BE POLITE billboard?

Full sunshine today. No thunderstorms chasing me from the west. *Bright, clear sky over a plain so wide.* I never did see or photograph a moving oil train, but I do see a westbound truck carrying the enormous blade of a wind turbine. And a minute later, another truck and another blade.

The world is moving on. If I turn my back on the past by selling my mineral rights to someone else, then I could move on, too. I would finally be free of complicity in the oil business, right?

Sure. Except for the synthetic fibers of the shirt I'm wearing, the plastic in the bag that holds the crumbs of yesterday's lunch, even the Vaseline I smear on my chapped lips. Petroleum Products R Us.

If I keep my mineral rights and honor the verve of my long-silent or forgotten ancestors who just wanted to get in on something on these vast plains, I would be able to afford more of the trips I love across this fine continent—and across the globe—courtesy of an engine invented, oh, a couple centuries ago when people rode horses and buggies, a machine that belches out carbon and trouble.

Sell the rights, keep the rights—my choices seem as distinct from each other as black and white, but after that, things quickly get murky.

ALEXANDRIA, MINNESOTA

Murky, or as my father would have said, interesting. When he packed up his big camera and scoured the countryside for old grain elevators and decrepit houses, and when he returned to his darkroom, he didn't worry about the limited palette of black and white. He found analytical delight in all of the elements that go into a satisfying composition—contrast, lighting, subtleties of tone, and line.

Does it make any sense to borrow the wisdom of my father to do something he probably never would have done?

ST. CLOUD, MINNESOTA

I take wisdom wherever I can find it.

If I look beyond black and white and pay attention to both the rich texture of my family history and the shadows cast by the drilling frenzy in North Dakota, I arrive at a decision I can live with: I plan to keep my mineral rights when they come to me, but send a sizable share of any royalty money I receive back to my father's home state, to people caught in the squeeze of high rents or to the natural areas threatened by oil development.

But the decision to keep my mineral rights, which means I will benefit financially from oil drilling, brings me little joy. With all these questions, I've been driving north in the southbound lane. Now I feel as though I'm driving south.

I-694 BELTWAY AROUND THE TWIN CITIES
My radio tells me that a runaway train carrying crude oil from North Dakota derailed in a small town in Quebec, and the contents exploded, several times. Fireball, five are dead so far, the downtown destroyed, forty people missing.

It sounds ghastly, and it doesn't make sense to me. Crude oil isn't supposed to be explosive. But then, trains aren't supposed to derail, pipelines aren't supposed to spill their contents, and tomorrow we will say North Dakota's drinking water isn't supposed to be tainted by oil-field activities. These things aren't supposed to happen.

Nothing like an explosion to remind me that I am still traveling in a dubious direction. How do I get off this road? How do *we* get off this road?

ADDENDUM

> Attached to and made a part of that certain con-
> tract dated _____ by and between _____ and
> _____. Regardless of language to the contrary in
> the contract to which this rider is attached, the
> following provisions shall take precedence over
> any terms in the contract.

> *An addendum is a change to a contract that both par-
> ties agree to make. It should be signed and executed
> with the same formality as the original contract.*

A DINING ROOM, IN THE NEAR FUTURE

Imagine a dining room table big enough to seat all of us. I'm
in this room, and so are you. We've got cups of coffee and
plates of cookies. We're here to haggle over the details of a
new agreement, which describes an energy policy as efficient
as the North Dakota wind and as direct as a North Dakota
farmer's gaze.

Because we're so good at haggling, we've been sitting at
this table a long time, but we're getting closer. Someone begins to read the latest draft:

> We agree on this ____ day of _____ to impose on any man-
> ufacturer, producer, or importer of a carbon polluting sub-
> stance a fee in accordance with this section.

The complicated sentences wind around and around the
room, but they make a simple point: fossil fuel causes pollution, myriad health ailments, and climate change. We agree
to add the cost of those problems to the fuels that cause
them. We agree to impose this cost—this tax—on fossil fuel

214

producers, but we also agree to rebate the revenue in a fair and equitable way to ourselves.

This agreement will lower carbon emissions on our big working playground—a continent that stretches from the Atlantic to the Pacific—and we will all benefit.

We know this policy will encourage us to use less of yesterday's high-carbon fuel and to live our lives in a less environmentally damaging way. We also know it will encourage our inventors to invent, and our investors to invest in, tomorrow's low-carbon technology. *Dazzle us!* we'll say. And they will.

By the time we sign this agreement and shake hands, stand up, stretch, and drift away from the table, the next boom—the solar boom   will be well under way. Solar technology could be so cheap, so everyday, we will buy it at Target.

I see a lot of wherefores and hereinafters in this contract and a lot more haggling, but I also see a way to get off the road we're on. I see hope.

MINNEAPOLIS, IN THE NEAR FUTURE

My young granddaughters and I are out for a late afternoon walk because it's snowing like crazy and they love snow. The three of us—descendants of prairie immigrants and homesteaders—know perfectly well how to dress for a snowstorm. We zip up our jackets and twirl our scarves around our necks as we approach the pedestrian bridge over the Mississippi River. The snowfall obscures the view of the downtown office towers, but we don't have to pass a rope from sleigh to sleigh to stay together. We just walk hand in hand.

Halfway across the bridge, we stop in a pool of light cast by one of the streetlights to watch the river rush over St. Anthony Falls.

You can see, I'm sure, how a walk across a snowy bridge with children is not exactly the time or place to talk about the family's North Dakota mineral rights. There will be time for that conversation later on, perhaps when these girls are old enough to get in on something that might be developing. I doubt it will have anything to do with oil. Someday I expect my granddaughters to give me one of those withering looks the younger generation reserves for its elders. *You* WHAT? *You used to drill holes two miles down and two miles across — for oil?* I can't wait for that day.

Meanwhile, I am fresh out of questions, but the children have plenty. *If we throw snowballs in the river, will we hit a fish? Are there fish? Why is that man riding a bicycle in the snow? Do you have any snacks in that bag?*

All this while the river flows beneath the bridge.

My father and I in Gainesville, Florida, 2002

ACKNOWLEDGMENTS

Many, many people helped me with this project, and I thank them all for their patience, generosity, and enthusiasm. Because the research for this book was a multi-state effort, I have organized my thank-yous by state.

In Wisconsin, thanks to:
Staff members and volunteers at the Crex Meadows Wildlife Area in Grantsburg for educating midwesterners about the beautiful flora and fauna of northwestern Wisconsin; Bruce Brown, geologist (retired) with the Wisconsin Geological and Natural History Survey, and Tom Woletz (retired) and Ruth King of the Wisconsin Department of Natural Resources for information about frac sand mining; and Dave Ferris, Burnett County conservationist, for offering information and perspective on the Grantsburg frac sand mine owned by Interstate Energy Partners and operated by Tiller Corporation.

In Iowa, thanks to:
Bob Eggen for his gracious tour of Swede Ridge and the Sny Magill Creek area in Clayton County; Michelle Pettit, McGregor Public Library, for getting me started on the Iowa leg of my research and letting me occupy her office for much of a day; the State Historical Society of Iowa for pointing me toward great references; and the Monona Historical Society for showing me their collection of historical photos and maps and for digging up hard-to-find evidence of my ancestors in Clayton County.

In Minnesota, thanks to:
T. J. for welcoming me to his home and farm so that I could see where my ancestors homesteaded; several historical soci-

eties—Stevens County, Douglas County, and the Minnesota Historical Society—for doing what they do best: keeping the past alive; James Olson, volunteer with the Swedish Genealogical Society of Minnesota, for finding the immigration records for my Swedish ancestors within a few minutes on just the right database; the University of Minnesota Wilson Library staff for unearthing Willa Cather's Lincoln (Nebraska) *Courier* reviews; Eunice Lake Dore and Janice Landis for sending information about the Swedish Jonssons and Anna Frisk; Sally Franson for teaching a creative nonfiction class at the Loft Literary Center with skill and irrepressible energy; trusted writing pals Susan Marie Swanson, Lindsay Johnson, Bridget Levin, and Rick Chrustowski for invaluable advice, for reading an early draft of the manuscript, and for helping me solve seemingly intractable literary problems; Ellen Qualey, law librarian at the University of Minnesota, for advice on legal definitions, and her mother, Marsha Qualey, for providing fresh eyes to a late draft; the Geological Society of Minnesota for its substantial contribution to my understanding of geology; David Fahlin for showing me the abandoned pioneer cemetery on land held by his family since the 1860s; Nancy Olsen for coming through at the last minute, once again, with great music ideas; Bob Walsh for photographic advice; Tony Runkel, chief geologist for the Minnesota Geological Survey, for answering frac sand questions; the Minnesota Genealogical Society for help in tracking down my Swedish ancestors; Richard Magraw, longtime friend and former St. Croix River neighbor, for letting me trespass on his property in order to visit my old river haunts; Byron Starns for generously agreeing to review legal concepts; and Kate Clover for being a fellow sand lover.

Special thanks goes to Ruth Johnson, a serious amateur historian who lives in my grandfather's hometown of Kensington and who helped me on numerous occasions. She sent me information I was unable to find anywhere else and took me on a tour of the countryside where the Westbergs farmed. She is a local treasure.

In North Dakota, thanks to:

Jim Davis and Emily Schultz and the entire staff of the State Historical Society of North Dakota in Bismarck for safeguarding priceless historical documents, for numerous trips into the secret stacks to fetch things for me, for mailing documents to my home, scanning photos, and answering questions I didn't know I had; Darren and Joan Gohrick, Leon and Larena McGinnity, Elaine Esterby, and LaVern Neff for their time, insights, and honesty; Ed Murphy, Stephan Nordeng, and Julie LeFever of the North Dakota Geological Survey for sharing their time, map skills, and knowledge about North Dakota oil; Darin Buri, F. D. Holland Geology Library manager, University of North Dakota, for showing me A. G. Leonard's frying pan from his camping trips; Dr. Joseph Hartman, paleontologist at the University of North Dakota, for looking hard for A. J. Collier's field notes; Curt Hanson and the staff at the Elwyn B. Robinson Department of Special Collections, Chester Fritz Library, University of North Dakota, for providing me with A. G. Leonard's 1917 field notes; the staff of the Williams County Recorder's office for cheerful, competent help; the staff of the Oil and Gas Division of the Department of Mineral Resources in the North Dakota Industrial Commission for straightforward explanations of mysterious oil issues; Andy Mork, Full Circle Geoscience, Boise, Idaho; David Fischer, independent geologist, Grand Forks, North Dakota; Jim Ryen, Williams County deputy auditor, Williston, North Dakota; and Joshua Swanson, attorney at Vogel Law Firm, Fargo, North Dakota, for their review of the manuscript or portions of the manuscript; and thanks, too, to a few North Dakotans who asked to remain anonymous and a few others whom I chose to keep anonymous to protect their privacy.

Special thanks goes to Monte Besler. The North Dakota oil industry has neither the time nor the inclination to stop drilling in order to answer a freelance writer's questions, which is one reason I was so grateful for Besler, hydraulic fracturing consultant in Williston. He showed interest in my writing project from the beginning, took time away from a full schedule to answer my questions, and gave me the upside-down canoe description. We disagree about climate change, but over the course of two years we conducted an extended conversation marked by mutual respect.

One last note about the North Dakotans: a few months after I talked to Leon McGinnity in 2013, he succumbed to cancer. Leon's experience and quiet wisdom were an inspiration to me. I send my best wishes to his family.

In my family, heartfelt thanks to:
The entire Westberg clan for a memorable trek across North Dakota to honor my father; Deb for digging up oil records, for listening, and for being my sister; my mother for her vivid memories of our family's past and for answering questions that only she could answer; Antonio for his photo advice and expertise; Bobby for his artistic contributions to the truck survey; Kip for his knowledge of the patent process; my daughters Emily and Anna for their kindness and understanding; and my young granddaughters Ingrid and Alba, two upstanding, and now fully upright, midwesterners who help make my life complete.

Special thanks to two others: Uncle Rich for his insights, for his sly humor, and for being so willing and eager to talk about the old days over the past three years, a debt I can't possibly repay; and to Dave for offering a husband's love and support and also a professional editor's eye and ear to this project from the very beginning.

And finally:
Grateful thanks to the entire staff at the Minnesota Historical Society Press. Thanks especially to Shannon Pennefeather and to Ann Regan, who applied diligence, passion, and smarts— Monday through Friday and often on the weekends—to my manuscript. Every writer needs a good editor or two, and after this experience I am a strong advocate of extending the "local" movement beyond food to include editors and publishers.

SOURCE NOTES

I began the research for this book soon after my father died in late 2011, and my research continued for the next two and a half years. I visited the Wisconsin frac sand mine near the St. Croix National Scenic Riverway in the spring of 2012. I traveled twice to western North Dakota, once in the summer of 2012 and again in the summer of 2013. In the spring of 2013, I visited the Mississippi River town of McGregor, Iowa, where my Swedish ancestors first landed, the farm country of west-central Minnesota, where they homesteaded, and my family's former property on the St. Croix. I combined all of these experiences into one narrative.

The chapter names in *Fractured Land* are derived from the clauses found in oil and gas leases, the specialized legal contracts between mineral owners and developers. The legal wording of each clause is followed by my translation in italics; in a few instances, I used definitions from *Black's Law Dictionary*, a respected source for legal terminology.

CONTRACT

Bryan A. Garner, *Black's Law Dictionary*, 10th ed. (Eagan, MN: Thomson Reuters, 2014).

▶ William Shemorry was a longtime newspaper photographer in Williston, North Dakota. He won many state and national photographic awards and was nominated for a Pulitzer Prize in 1967. One of his proudest achievements must have been the photo he took of the North Dakota oil discovery well in 1951. For more information about Bill Shemorry, see the State Historical Society of North Dakota's website:
    http://history.nd.gov/archives/manuscripts/inventory/10958 .html.

▶ Over the course of his career, my father was awarded seven patents; he collaborated with other 3M scientists on six of the seven.

The first two (including the brassiere) involved nonwoven fabrics, the third was a photographic film–cleaning fabric, and the last four were anti-static products.

▶ For more information about the latest and largest North Dakota oil boom, see:

Eric Konigsberg, "Kuwait on the Prairie: Can North Dakota Solve the Energy Problem?" *The New Yorker* (April 25, 2011),
    http://www.newyorker.com/reporting/2011/04/25/110425fa
    _fact_konigsberg?currentPage=all.

Steven Mufson, "In North Dakota, the Gritty Side of an Oil Boom," *Washington Post,* July 8, 2012,
    http://www.washingtonpost.com/business/economy/in-north
    -dakota-the-gritty side of-an-oil-boom/2012/07/18/gJQAZ
    k5ZuW_story.html.

Chip Brown, "North Dakota Went Boom," *New York Times Magazine* (January 31, 2013),
    http://www.nytimes.com/2013/02/03/magazine/north-dakota
    -went-boom.html?_r=0.

Edwin Dobb, "The New Oil Landscape: The Fracking Frenzy in North Dakota Has Boosted the U.S. Fuel Supply—But at What Cost?" *National Geographic* (March 2013),
    http://ngm.nationalgeographic.com/2013/03/bakken-shale-oi
    l/dobb-text.

"A Tale of Two Rushes: There's Gold in Them There Wells," *The Economist,* December 21, 2013,
    http://www.economist.com/news/christmas-specials/21591748
    -theres-gold-them-there-wells.

Todd Melby, lead producer, "Black Gold Boom," a web and radio series exploring the oil boom in western North Dakota:
    http://blackgoldboom.com/.

▶ In 2008, the U.S. Geological Survey issued an estimate of oil reserves in the Bakken Formation:

Richard M. Pollastro, Troy A. Cook, Laura N. R. Roberts, Christopher J. Schenk, Michael D. Lewan, Lawrence O. Anna, Stephanie B. Gaswirth, Paul G. Lillis, Timothy R. Klett, and Ronald R. Charpentier, "Assessment of Undiscovered Oil Resources in the Devonian-Mississippian Bakken Formation, Williston Basin Province, Montana and North Dakota, 2008," U.S. Geological Survey, April 2008,

http://pubs.usgs.gov/fs/2008/3021/pdf/FS08-3021_508.pdf.

▶ In 2013, the U.S. Geological Survey issued a much higher estimate of oil in two formations, the Bakken and the Three Forks, in the Williston Basin:

Stephanie B. Gaswirth, Kristen R. Marra, Troy A. Cook, Ronald R. Charpentier, Donald L. Gautier, Debra K. Higley, Timothy R. Klett, Michael D. Lewan, Paul G. Lillis, Christopher J. Schenk, Marilyn E. Tennyson, and Katherine J. Whidden, "Assessment of Undiscovered Oil Resources in the Bakken and Three Forks Formations, Williston Basin Province, Montana, North Dakota, and South Dakota, 2013," U.S. Geological Survey, April 2013,

http://pubs.usgs.gov/fs/2013/3013/fs2013-3013.pdf.

▶ For national statistics and analyses relating to oil and all forms of energy, see the extensive website of the Energy Information Administration, a federal agency:

http://www.eia.gov/.

BONUS

▶ The illustration of North Dakota's first oil "pool" was published about a half year after oil was discovered in commercial quantities in North Dakota: "Outline of First Oil Pool to Be Defined in N.D.," *Fargo Forum*, November 29, 1951.

▶ For more information about the Victory ships, see:

Frederic Chapin Lane, *Ships for Victory: A History of Shipbuilding under the U.S. Maritime Commission in World War II* (Baltimore, MD: Johns Hopkins University Press, 2001). Or go to this link:

http://www.globalsecurity.org/military/systems/ship/victory -ships-design.htm.

PRIMARY TERM

▶ I consulted the following sources to learn about North Dakota oil leasing: well operators (the oil and gas companies), fellow mineral rights owners, mineral owners' forums online, and the Oil and Gas Division of the Department of Mineral Resources in the North Dakota Industrial Commission. The following two references were also very helpful:

Ron Anderson, "North Dakota Oil & Gas Leasing Considerations," *Extension Bulletin* 29 (Fargo: Cooperative Extension Service, North Dakota State University, November 1981, rev. 2006),

https://www.dmr.nd.gov/oilgas/leasingconsiderations.pdf.

Joshua A. Swanson, "The Fine Print Matters: Negotiating an Oil and Gas Lease in North Dakota," *North Dakota Law Review* 87.4 (December 2011): 709.

▶ For more information about midwestern frac sand mining, see:

"Frac Sand Fever," an occasional (Minneapolis) *Star Tribune* series on the frac sand mining boom in Minnesota and Wisconsin:

http://www.startribune.com/local/177697161.html.

▶ One of several articles about the Grantsburg frac sand mine spill:

Kelly Smith, "Wisconsin Sues Twin Cities Firms over Sand Spill in the St. Croix River," (Minneapolis) *Star Tribune*, June 9, 2012,

http://www.startribune.com/local/west/158319005.html.

GRANTING CLAUSE

▶ The passages about the Scandinavian American homesteader Per Hansa came from this stirring classic:

O. E. Rølvaag, *Giants in the Earth* (New York and London: Harper and Brothers Publishers, 1927).

▶ The following were among the resources I consulted to learn more about the history of North Dakota:

Elwyn B. Robinson, *History of North Dakota* (Lincoln: University of Nebraska Press, 1966).

Larry Remele, "Summary of History of North Dakota" *North Dakota Blue Book* (Bismarck: State Historical Society of North Dakota, 1989). This work also appears on the historical society's website: http://www.history.nd.gov/ndhistory/summaryintro.html.

▶ Excerpts from the journals of the Lewis and Clark expedition came from a website sponsored by the National Endowment for the Humanities, the Center for Great Plains Studies, the University of Nebraska Center for Digital Research in the Humanities, and University of Nebraska Press: http://lewisandclarkjournals.unl.edu/.

The full text of Meriwether Lewis's journal entry on April 19, 1805, when the explorers were camped in Williams County, North Dakota, reads:

The wind blew So hard this morning from N. W. that we dared not to venture our canoes on the river. — Observed considerable quantities of dwarf Juniper on the hill sides (see specimen No. 4) it seldom rises higher then 3 feet. — the wind detained us through the couse of this day, tho' we were fortunate in having placed ourselves in a safe harbour. the party killed one Elk and a beaver today. The beaver of this part of the Missouri are larger, fatter, more abundant and better clad with fur than those of any other part of the country that I have yet seen; I have remarked also that their fur is much darker. —
    http://lewisandclarkjournals.unl.edu/read/?_xmlsrc=1805 -04-19.xml&_xslsrc=LCstyles.xsl.

IMPLIED COVENANTS

Henry Campbell Black, *A Law Dictionary Containing Definitions of the Terms and Phrases of American and English Jurisprudence, Ancient and Modern*, 2nd ed. (St. Paul, MN: West Publishing Co., 1910), http://thelawdictionary.org/

▶ For information on Swedish emigration in the 1860s, I consulted:

Franklin D. Scott, *Sweden: The Nation's History* (Minneapolis: University of Minnesota Press, 1977).

Anne Gillespie Lewis, *Swedes in Minnesota* (St. Paul: Minnesota Historical Society Press, 2004).

June Drenning Holmquist, ed., *They Chose Minnesota: A Survey of the State's Ethnic Groups* (St. Paul: Minnesota Historical Society Press, 1981).

Lars Ljungmark, *For Sale—Minnesota: Organized Promotion of Scandinavian Immigration 1866–1873* (Chicago: The Swedish Pioneer Historical Society, 1971).

H. Arnold Barton, ed., *Clipper Ship and Covered Wagon: Essays from the Swedish Pioneer Historical Quarterly* (New York: Arno Press, 1979).

H. Arnold Barton, *Letters from the Promised Land: Swedes in America, 1840–1914* (Minneapolis: University of Minnesota Press, 2000).

▶ For information on Swedish American settlers, I consulted:

Centennial Book Committee, *Hoffman Centennial 1891–1991: My Home Town* (Hoffman, MN: The committee, 1991).

Arthur J. Larsen, "Roads and Trails in the Minnesota Triangle, 1849–60," *Minnesota History* 11.4 (December 1930): 387–411,

> http://collections.mnhs.org/MNHistoryMagazine/articles/11
> /v11i04p387-411.pdf.

Girart Hewitt, *Minnesota: Its Advantages to Settlers 1868* (St. Paul: The author, 1868).

Hans Mattson, *The New Swedish Colony in Minnesota—North America, Good Land for Emigrants, at the Cheapest Conditions by [the] Lake Superior Railway* (Kristianstad: K. J. M. Mollersvard, 1872).

MNopedia, a website sponsored by the Minnesota Historical Society, http://www.mnopedia.org/person/mattson-hans-1832-1893.

George T. Flom, "The Early Swedish Immigration to Iowa," *Iowa Journal of History and Politics* 3.4 (October 1905): 583–615,

> https://archive.org/stream/iowajournalofhis03stat#page/n5
> /mode/2up.

Realto E. Price, ed., *History of Clayton County, Iowa: From the Earliest Historical Times Down to the Present* (Chicago: Robert O. Law Co., 1916),

> https://openlibrary.org/books/OL22882361M/History_of
> _Clayton_County_Iowa.

History of Clayton County Iowa 1882 (Chicago: Inter-State Publishing Company, 1882).

▶ This website contains a discussion of the founding of Swedish and Norwegian immigrant churches in Clayton County, Iowa:

   http://boards.ancestry.com/thread.aspx?mv=flat&m=28&p
   =topics.religious.lutheran.lutheran-clergy.

POOLING

▶ *National Geographic*'s 2008 article about North Dakota:

Charles Bowden, "The Emptied Prairie," *National Geographic* (January 2008),

   http://ngm.nationalgeographic.com/2008/01/emptied-north
   -dakota/bowden-text.

▶ And North Dakota governor John Hoeven's response:

"Hoeven Responds to National Geographic Story," *Bismarck Tribune,* January 13, 2008,

   http://bismarcktribune.com/news/local/hoeven-responds
   -to-national-geographic-story/article_900d192c-73b5-5d1e
   -baa8-54456942991f.html.

▶ Reading one-hundred-year-old editions of *The Alamo Farmer* at the state archives in Bismarck is where I almost overcame my hatred for microfilm machines. I found ads for the new J. J. Westberg & Son hardware store in several issues of *The Alamo Farmer.* "Son" referred to my grandfather's brother, Edwin.

The highly optimistic article on Alamo's future:

"Alamo, The Queen City of Stanley-Grenora R. R.: Opportunities in Evidence Surpass Anything Ever Seen in an Agricultural Community in the Northwest," *The Alamo Farmer,* November 3, 1916.

▶ I found the turn-of-the-twentieth-century newspaper advertisements for land in North Dakota in the *Morris (Minnesota) Sun.*

▶ A two-volume tome offers many North Dakota homesteader stories and was the first source to reveal to me my grandfather's homesteading past:

Marlene Eide, coord., *The Wonder of Williams: A History of Williams County, North Dakota* (N.p.: Williams County Historical Society, 1975).

▶ I consulted the Bureau of Land Management's General Land Office Records website to find out where and when my ancestors homesteaded:

http://www.glorecords.blm.gov/.

▶ For information on the early history of oil exploration in North Dakota, I read:

John P. Bluemle, *The 50th Anniversary of the Discovery of Oil in North Dakota, Miscellaneous Series No. 89* (Bismarck: North Dakota Geological Survey, 2001).

John P. Bluemle, *The First 100 Years: The History of the North Dakota Geological Survey 1895–1995, Miscellaneous Series No. 81* (Bismarck: North Dakota Geological Survey, 1996).

A. J. Collier, "The Nesson Anticline: Williams County, North Dakota Bulletin 691-G," *Contributions to Economic Geology* (Washington, DC: Government Printing Office, 1918).

▶ Two handwritten documents:

A. J. Collier, letter to A. G. Leonard, January 4, 1918, and A. G. Leonard, Ray Quadrangle Field Notes, North Dakota Geological Survey, Grand Forks, ND, 1917–18, Elwyn B. Robinson Department of Special Collections, Chester Fritz Library, University of North Dakota, Grand Forks.

FORCE MAJEURE CLAUSE

▶ I learned about my grandfather's and great-grandfather's business and financial failings in Williams County district court documents provided by the State Historical Society of North Dakota.

▶ One of the news accounts of my great-grandfather's fatal accident:

"New Death Brings Motor Toll to 20," *Minneapolis Journal,* May 14, 1926.

MOTHER HUBBARD CLAUSE

▶ The full text of the Lewis and Clark journal entry from April 21, 1805, reads:

Set out an early hour this morning. Capt Clark walked on shore; the wind tho' head was not violent. the country through which we passed is very simelar in every rispect to that through which we have passed for several days. - We saw immence herds of buffaloe Elk deer & antelopes. we reached the place of incampment after dark, which was on the Lard. side a little above White earth river." (Scholars consider this a reference to the Little Muddy River, which empties into the Missouri River near Williston.)

> http://lewisandclarkjournals.unl.edu/read/?_xmlsrc=1805 -04-21.xml&_xslsrc=LCstyles.xsl.

▶ To learn about the Mother Hubbard clause, I consulted:

Wesley Fain, "Expansive Capabilities of 'Mother Hubbard Clause' Key for Resource Play Leases," *The American Oil and Gas Reporter* (December 2011),

> http://www.aogr.com/index.php/web-features/exclusive-story /expansive-capabilities-of-mother-hubbard-clause-key-for -resource-leases.

Bryan A. Garner, *A Dictionary of Modern Legal Usage* (New York: Oxford University Press, 2001).

▶ In addition to works previously cited, the following references helped me piece together North Dakota oil history from the 1920s through the 1940s:

"The Big Viking Goes Down After Oil. You Ask for Action—Here It Is!" full-page advertisement, *Williams County Farmers Press*, March 28, 1928.

"Big Viking Oil Meeting," advertisement, *Williston Herald*, October 24, 1929.

"Big Viking to Increase Stock: Company's Capital to Be Raised to 500,000 Shares to Provide Further Working Funds," *Williston Herald*, February 14, 1930.

"Drilling Operations Halted at Well," *Ray Pioneer*, September 1, 1938.

Well log of the Nels Kamp #1 operated by the California Company, Thomas Leach Papers, State Historical Society of North Dakota, Bismarck.

William Shemorry, *Mud, Sweat and Oil: The Early Days of the Williston Basin* (Williston, ND: The author, 1991).

A. G. Leonard, "Possibilities of Oil and Gas in North Dakota, Bulletin No. 1," North Dakota Geological Survey, 1920.

"Oil Driller is Sure Nesson Dome O.K.," *Williams County Farmers Press*, January 18, 1928.

Advertisement, Big Viking Oil Company, *Williams County Farmers Press*, March 28, 1928.

Advertisement, Big Viking Oil Company, *Williams County Farmers Press*, October 24, 1929.

"Big Viking to Increase Stock," *Williston Herald*, February 14, 1930.

"Crew Left City Today," *Ray Pioneer*, September 8, 1938.

▶ For information on specific wells, I consulted the North Dakota Oil and Gas Division website:
   https://www.dmr.nd.gov/oilgas/.

▶ Information about the first commercial hydraulic fracturing came from the American Oil and Gas Historical Society:
   http://aoghs.org/technology/shooters-well-fracking-history/.

▶ The following article convinced me that my grandfather had bought land on the Nesson Anticline in the hope of striking oil:

"Major Companies Will Drill for Oil: Nesson Structure Being Leased for Development," *Williams County Farmers Press*, January 23, 1941.

ASSIGNMENT

"Oscar Westberg Dies Suddenly," *Williston Herald and Farmers Press*, April 24, 1956.

"3 Killed in Wreck Near Stanley," *Williston Herald*, June 23, 2013.

ROYALTY CLAUSE

▶ To learn more about 3M's innovative process leading to a highly profitable line of disposable face masks, and my father's contributions to it, I read documents contained in my father's extensive files and the following:

"How Four Companies Spawn New Products By Encouraging Risks: Failures Are Part of Game; Proposals Are Welcome From the Customers, Too: Safety Mask from Brassiere," *Wall Street Journal*, September 18, 1980.

"One Man's Idea Sparked 3M Successes," *Minneapolis Star*, September 8, 1981.

A Century of Innovation, the 3M Story (St. Paul, MN: 3M Co., 2002).

Maggie Overfelt, "The Square Pegs: To Keep Its Chief Tapehead Happy, 3M Gave Him His Own Innovation Greenhouse, Where He and Other Misfits Developed a String of Hits," *Fortune Small Business*, reprinted on cnn.com, April 1, 2003,
    http://money.cnn.com/magazines/fsb/fsb_archive/2003/04/01 /341017/.

▶ This article described my trip to Washington, DC, to protest the Vietnam War:

"7 R.F. Students Go to D.C. Peace Rally," *Student Voice* (Wisconsin State University–River Falls), April 26, 1971.

▶ For more information on the national Wild and Scenic Rivers System, see:
    http://www.rivers.gov/.

▶ My essay about the proposed freeway bridge across the St. Croix River:

"An Eyesore, Used to Justify Another One," (Minneapolis) *Star Tribune*, September 9, 2011.

REWORKING OPERATIONS

Family letters.

INDEMNITY CLAUSE

▶ For more information about hydraulic fracturing, see:

Department of Energy, Hydraulic Fracturing White Paper, June 2004, http://www.epa.gov/ogwdw/uic/pdfs/cbmstudy_attach_uic _append_a_doe_whitepaper.pdf.

U.S. Geological Survey, "USGS Frequently Asked Questions," http://www.usgs.gov/faq/?q=taxonomy/term/10132.

Environmental Protection Agency, "The Process of Hydraulic Fracturing," http://www2.epa.gov/hydraulicfracturing/process-hydraulic -fracturing.

National Geographic interactive feature on hydraulic fracturing: http://news.nationalgeographic.com/news/2010/10/101022 -breaking-fuel-from-the-rock/.

Sierra Club, Beyond Natural Gas campaign, http://content.sierraclub.org/naturalgas/.

"Hydraulic Fracturing: An Environmentally Responsible Technology for Ensuring Our Energy Future," from Baker Hughes Incorporated, an oil-field services company, http://assets.cmp.bh.mxmcloud.com/system/3881f7d82 b144e186e83ddald867b3e5_34988.Hydraulic-Fracturing_White -Paper.0212.pdf.

FracFocus: This website began as a voluntary registry for the chemicals used in hydraulic fracturing. Some states now require well operators to list the chemicals used in the fracking process on FracFocus, and North Dakota is one of them. There are as yet no federal regulations requiring well operators to disclose all chemicals. http://fracfocus.org/hydraulic-fracturing-how-it-works /hydraulic-fracturing-process.

▶ A technical paper about North Dakota–style fracking:

C. Mark Pearson, Larry Griffin, Chris Wright (Liberty Resources), and Leen Weijers (Liberty Oilfield Services), "Breaking Up Is Hard to Do: Creating Hydraulic Fracture Complexity in the Bakken Central Basin," Conference Paper, Society of Professional Engineers

Hydraulic Fracturing Technology Conference, the Woodlands, TX, February 4–6, 2013,

> http://www.libertyresourcesllc.com/files/SPE_163827_Final .pdf.

▶ I read several books about the domestic energy boom triggered by horizontal drilling and hydraulic fracturing:

Russell Gold, *The Boom: How Fracking Ignited the American Energy Revolution and Changed the World* (New York: Simon and Schuster, 2014). The author devotes a chapter ("Everyone Comes for the Money") to his observations of a hydraulic fracturing operation near Killdeer, North Dakota.

Gregory Zuckerman, *The Frackers: The Outrageous Inside Story of the New Billionaire Wildcatters* (New York: Portfolio Hardcover, 2013). This book focuses on the industry's risk-takers and innovators, including those who devised a successful drilling formula for the Bakken Shale.

Tom Wilber, *Under the Surface: Fracking, Fortunes, and the Fate of the Marcellus Shale* (Ithaca, NY: Cornell University Press, 2012). A reporter's examination of the communities affected by the natural gas boom in Pennsylvania's Marcellus Shale.

Seamus McGraw, *The End of Country: Dispatches from the Frack Zone* (New York: Random House, 2011). The author describes how the boom in natural gas drilling in the Marcellus Shale affected his family and a Pennsylvania community.

▶ For more information about oil development on the Fort Berthold Reservation:

"Tribe Breaks Ground on Refinery," Oil Patch Dispatch, *Fargo Forum,* May 9, 2013,

> http://oilpatchdispatch.areavoices.com/2013/05/09/tribe -breaks-ground-on-refinery/.

Richard Nemec, "North Dakota Reservation Awash in Oil, Energy Ideas," *MHA Nation News,* April 28, 2014,

> http://www.mhanation.com/main2/Home_News/Home_News _2014/News_2014_04_April/news_2014_april_28_north_dakota _reservation_awash_in_oil_energy_ideas.html.

▶ For more information about the history and formation of oil in the Bakken Shale:

Stephan Nordeng, "The Bakken Petroleum System: An Example of a Continuous Petroleum Accumulation," *Geo News*, North Dakota Department of Mineral Resources Newsletter (January 2009),

https://www.dmr.nd.gov/ndgs/documents/newsletter/2009 Winter/PDF/BakkenPetroleum.pdf.

Stephan Nordeng, "A Brief History of Oil Production from the Bakken Formation in the Williston Basin," *Geo News*, North Dakota Department of Mineral Resources Newsletter (January 2010),

https://www.dmr.nd.gov/ndgs/documents/newsletter/nl2010 /ABriefHistoryofOilProductionfromtheBakkenFormation intheWillistonBasin.pdf.

SECONDARY TERM

▶ I found information about Zhu Hsi (alternative spelling, Chu Hsi) in:

Charlotte Horlyck, "Confucian Burial Practices in the Late Goryeo and Early Joseon Periods," *Review of Korean Studies* 11.2 (Republic of Korea: Academy of Korean Studies, June 2008).

Chu Hsi's Family Rituals: A Twelfth-Century Chinese Manual for the Performance of Cappings, Weddings, Funerals and Ancestral Rites, trans. Patricia Buckley Ebrey (Princeton, NJ: Princeton University Press, 1991).

▶ My father played the English horn solo in the second movement of Anton Dvorak's Symphony No. 9 in E Minor (*New World Symphony*) for the 3M Symphony Orchestra on February 29, 1976, in the Janet Wallace Auditorium at Macalester College in St. Paul.

▶ The Pulitzer Prize–winning American writer Willa Cather heard Antonin Dvorak's *New World Symphony* shortly after the Czech composer wrote it in the early 1890s. She wrote a review of the symphony for the December 25, 1897, edition of the *Courier* in Lincoln, Nebraska. I read Cather's review in *The World and the Parish, Volume One: Willa Cather's Articles and Reviews 1893–1902*, ed. William M. Curtin (Lincoln: University of Nebraska Press, 2002). She wrote about the symphony again in the voice of Thea Kronberg, the main character in her novel *The Song of the Lark* (Boston and New York: Houghton Mifflin Company, 1915 and 1943).

IN WITNESS WHEREOF

Bryan A. Garner, *Black's Law Dictionary,* 10th ed. (Eagan, MN: Thomson Reuters, 2014).

▶ For more information on climate change, see:

The website of the National Oceanic and Atmospheric Administration: http://www.noaa.gov/climate.html.

The National Aeronautics and Space Administration website includes information aimed at children and educators: http://climate.nasa.gov/.

The University Corporation for Atmospheric Research, a consortium of more than one hundred colleges and universities, focuses on research and training in atmospheric and earth sciences: https://www2.ucar.edu/news/backgrounders/understanding -climate-change-global-warming.

In 2013, the Intergovernmental Panel on Climate Change issued its Fifth Assessment Report on the current state of climate change science: https://www.ipcc.ch/report/ar5/wg1/.

▶ For more information on how climate change is affecting the Midwest, see:

Environmental Protection Agency, "Climate Impacts in the Midwest," http://www.epa.gov/climatechange/impacts-adaptation /midwest.html.

ADDENDUM

▶ The language in the imagined dining room of the near future comes from carbon tax legislation introduced by Senators Barbara Boxer (D-California) and Bernie Sanders (I-Vermont) in 2013, http://www.sanders.senate.gov/imo/media/doc/0121413 -ClimateProtectionAct.pdf.

▶ Congress has so far blocked President Obama's efforts to pass an emissions tax, an approach to reducing carbon emissions favored by most economists. In June 2014, Obama and the U.S. Environmental Protection Agency proposed rules to cut carbon pollution from the nation's power plants. For more information, see:

"Clean Power Plan Overview,"

    http://www2.epa.gov/carbon-pollution-standards/fact-sheet -clean-power-plan-overview.

▶ For impartial, nonpartisan information on the concept of a carbon tax, see:

"Effects of a Carbon Tax on the Economy and the Environment," Congressional Budget Office, May 2013,

    http://www.cbo.gov/sites/default/files/cbofiles/attachments /44223_Carbon_0.pdf.

Donald Marron and Eric Toder, "Carbon Taxes and Corporate Tax Reform," The Urban Institute and Urban-Brookings Tax Policy Center, February 11, 2013,

    http://www.taxpolicycenter.org/UploadedPDF/412744 -Carbon-Taxes-and-Corporate-Tax-Reform.pdf.

Brad Plumer, "What's the Best Way to Design a Carbon Tax? Lawmakers Ask for Suggestions," washingtonpost.com, March 13, 2013,

    http://www.washingtonpost.com/blogs/wonkblog/wp/2013 /03/13/lawmakers-unveil-a-choose-your-own-adventure -carbon-tax/?wprss=rss_ezra-klein.

fractured land

was designed and set in type by Judy Gilats in St. Paul, Minnesota. The text face is Escrow and the display face is Gotham. The book was printed by Versa Press in East Peoria, Illinois.